CRYING AT MOVIES

CRYING AT MOVIES

A MEMOIR

JOHN MANDERINO

Academy Chicago Publishers

Published in 2008 by
Academy Chicago Publishers
363 West Erie Street
Chicago, Illinois 60610

Printed in the U.S.A.

Library of Congress Cataloging-in-Publication Data

Manderino, John.
  Crying at movies : a memoir / John Manderino.
    p. cm.
  ISBN 978-0-89733-580-5 (pbk.)
  1. Manderino, John. 2. Authors, American--20th century—Biography.
3. Motion pictures—Psychological aspects. I. Title.

  PS3563.A46387Z46 2008
  813'.54—dc22
  [B]
                              2008037434

To Marie

CONTENTS

DEATH OF THE DINOSAURS

I remember, Aunt Sarah took me and my cousin Gene. I was six. Gene was eight and knew all about dinosaurs. He had little rubber ones in his room and knew their long names, their attitudes and eating habits. And while I sat there in my thick red seat, gazing at the blank screen, he whispered in my ear that no one knew why the dinosaurs all died out but this movie would explain what happened.

The lights lowered.

Dinosaurs, huge and steamy and sluggish, roamed among palm trees and giant ferns. Gene leaned his head near mine. "That's a brontosaurus," he whispered. And: "That's a tyrannosaur." And: "That's not a bird, that's a pterodactyl."

Meanwhile, a man's deep smooth voice was telling us how contented the dinosaurs were, what a good life they had. Most of them were plant eaters. Some, it's true, ate other dinosaurs, but that was all right. Peaceful music played on.

Then the music darkened.

Something bad was going to happen.

Then it happened.

Volcanoes blew their lids, the music exploding, and thick boiling lava came oozing down, spreading everywhere, picking up speed, moving swifter than the dinosaurs could flee, some sinking into it, bellowing, others galloping through the smoke and falling flakes, their bodies on fire, howling like huge dogs. And the volcanoes caused earthquakes, opening long jagged cracks in the ground, one of them running right between a dinosaur's feet, and he spread his legs while the crack grew wider until he couldn't stretch any further and fell in, roaring with horror.

I couldn't take this. I was crying. I wanted out. Aunt Sarah took me into the lobby.

It was quiet out there, clean red carpeting everywhere. I sat on a padded bench while she went to the glass concession stand and returned with a box of popcorn to settle my nerves.

But I was so shaky I dropped the box, popcorn tumbling out on the beautiful clean carpet. I got down on my hands and knees and began quickly picking up kernels and putting them back in the box, an usher coming in a red coat and tie, swinging a big-headed flashlight.

He stood over me. I waited on my hands and knees, head hung, hoping whatever he was going to do he would do it quickly. He spoke to Aunt Sarah, who was sitting there smoking a cigarette. "Nice boy," he said.

"My sister's kid."

He bent down to me, hands on his knees. "Would you like another box of popcorn, fella?"

I looked up at him. He had thick dark hair in his nose. "No, thank you." I didn't want any popcorn. I just wanted to go home.

The usher patted me on the head, good dog, and went away.

I sat next to Aunt Sarah and chewed linty popcorn while she smoked another Lucky Strike and told me not to worry, it was only a movie, and anyway it all happened millions of years ago.

I could still faintly hear the dinosaurs bellowing away in there. They were so huge and pitiful. It seemed hard to believe that God would allow such a horrible thing to actually happen. But there it was, on film.

I wondered what else He would allow to happen.

THE SANDS OF IWO JIMA

"That's real footage," Uncle Doug points out.

It's a grainy, faraway shot of a Marine hosing down a hillside with a flame-thrower.

I say to him, "Huh."

Then it's back to John Wayne and his men, who seem far more real than the real footage. John Wayne is Sergeant Stryker, his men the men of Company Able, on an island with palm trees, white beaches, and "a whole lot of little lemon-colored fellas," as Stryker puts it.

Japs, he means.

I'm in my pajamas sitting cross-legged on a throw rug, my younger brother Mike upstairs in bed, Uncle Doug behind me in his sofa chair, in my parents' basement where he lives.

Uncle Doug resembles Sergeant Stryker. He's my mom's brother so he's not Italian and he looks like a combination of John Wayne, President Kennedy and the Marlboro Man.

"That's called a B.A.R., what that guy is using right there," he says.

I know he's waiting for me to ask him, so I do: "What's that stand for?"

"Browning automatic rifle."

"Huh."

Uncle Doug knows a lot about the war, having been in it. So was my dad, but Uncle Doug was a machine gunner on Okinawa. My dad was a cook on an island off Alaska—we have pictures of him, smiling, wearing the same white apron he wears at the butcher shop, not wearing a helmet, not needing one.

"Uncle Doug?"

"Uh-huh?"

"Did you kill any Japs over there?"

He tells me that isn't something you should talk about. "But I'll tell you this," he says. "I know for sure I got at least eighteen of those sons-a-bitches—possibly more, but eighteen for certain. But like I said, it's not something you should talk about."

"Eighteen, Uncle Doug?"

"At least."

My dad killed pigs and chickens.

"Those boats are called A.L.C.'s," Uncle Doug informs me.

"A.L.C.?"

"Amphibious landing craft."

"Huh."

Stryker and his men hit the beach but get pinned down.

This wisecracking Brooklyn Dodger fan they call Rigs gets shot. He tells Stryker, "Looks like . . . I'll get a good . . . night's sleep . . . tonight, Sarge," and dies.

Then a commercial for Bill Moran, your friendly Dodge dealer. "C'mon down!" he shouts, spreading his arms.

Rigs is dead and this clown is selling cars.

I sit there wishing to God I was on Iwo Jima with a B.A.R., racing in a zigzag, blazing away, screaming, *Die, you lemon-colored sons-a-bitches, die, die!*

"Absolutely worst cars ever built," Uncle Doug is telling me.

He drives a Plymouth Fury. It's parked out front, a work helmet in the back window. When he's not between jobs he's an ironworker, in a helmet and tool belt, strolling sky-high girders, a Pall Mall in the corner of his mouth.

My dad wears an apron and waits on customers. He doesn't even smoke.

"That's a good old standard M-1 rifle he's got right there," Uncle Doug points out when the movie is back, Stryker shooting a Jap who shot the happy-go-lucky guy from Tennessee they called Farmer.

"Huh."

I'm not that sorry about Farmer. He was kind of an idiot.

Stryker and his men fight their way to Mount Suribachi, where they rest for a minute, Stryker pulling out his cigarettes, saying he feels pretty good. And just then, just as he's saying how good he feels, he gets a bullet in the back from a sniper.

Someone machine-guns a nearby palm tree and a Jap falls out of it. Then they turn to Stryker. "Is he . . . ?" one of the men says. And the one bending over the body says, "Yeah."

"Those bastards," Uncle Doug says quietly.

I can't speak.

Then that famous shot of those five Marines raising the American flag on Mount Suribachi.

"That's real footage."

I manage to say, "Huh," tears running freely down my face now.

Then one of the men growls out, "All right, let's get back in the war." And they trudge off.

The End, music up:

From the halls of Montezu-uma
To the shores of Tripoli . . .

Uncle Doug tells me to turn it off and I do, but I don't want to leave. I want to talk. I want to tell him how I feel about the United States Marine Corps, whose motto is *Semper Fidelis*, meaning *Always Faithful*, and how faithful I will be to the Marines, always, and how I hope to God when I'm old enough to enlist there's a war going on, hopefully with those little lemon-colored bastards again.

But he tells me, "Lights out, soldier."

I go upstairs. I walk quietly past my parents' bedroom, my dad snoring away in there.

He has to get up at 5:30 in the morning, while it's still dark out. And he doesn't get home again until dark. And he does that six days a week, for us—my mom and me and my brother and three sisters—and I know he's the best father in the world. I know that. I do.

But still: while all those guys were dying on Iwo Jima—guys like Rigs, like Stryker—he was up in Alaska, in an apron, making spaghetti and meatballs.

RIO BRAVO

There was this very clean, very quiet kid my age, Jerome Fitzgerald, who lived at the other end of the block with just his mom. One rainy Saturday afternoon he rang our front doorbell. My mother answered it and came for me. "It's that kid—what's his name? Jerome?"

"Who?"

"From down the block."

"What's *he* want?" I said, going to see.

He was standing on the porch in a yellow raincoat and hood, under an umbrella. He spoke as if reciting: "My mother was wondering if you would like to come with me to see a movie at the Dolton Theater. Not with her," he added. "She'll just drive."

Out on the street a car was parked along the curb, its motor running, a large woman behind the wheel.

"Right now, you mean?" I asked.

"Yes," he said.

"What movie?"

"*Thunderball.*"

"James Bond?"

He nodded.

I stood there considering.

"Is she paying?" I asked.

He nodded.

"What about candy?"

He nodded.

I told him that sounded fine. I went and got my raincoat.

On the way there, I sat with Jerome in the back seat, his mother explaining as she drove along, "You looked to me like the sort of fellow who might enjoy seeing a good movie now and then—Jerome's the same way, the very same—and I thought to myself, 'Now isn't it silly—isn't it *selfish*—to be taking only one of these boys to the movies, just because he happens to be my son?'"

I looked at Jerome.

He shrugged.

As it turned out, the movie was quite excellent, and during it I had two bags of popcorn, a box of Good 'n' Plenty, a large Coke, and a Slo-Poke which I was still working on as we afterwards got into her car waiting out front.

"Well? How was it? How was it?"

I told her it was good.

"Jerome? *Your* verdict?"

He told her he thought it was good, too.

"Great minds think alike," she said, and laughed, pulling away from the curb.

On the way home she talked about how wonderfully this had worked out and said we should do this every time a new movie came to the theater, on its very first Saturday matinee. "What do you think, John? Does that sound to you like a pretty good idea?"

I told her, "Sure."

"Jerome? What about you? John is up for it. Do you think that sounds like a pretty good idea? Pretty good plan?"

"I guess," he said, looking out his window.

She laughed. "Great minds think alike!"

Turning down our street she asked me if I would like to stop over for some fudge brownies she'd made especially.

I didn't want any. For one thing, I was so full I wasn't sure I could finish my Slo-Poke. And anyway I didn't want to go to Jerome's house. He was so quiet and she never shut up. "No, thank you," I said. "I'm supposed to be doing something."

"Oh?" she said.

"I'm building a doll house for my little sister Nancy."

"How sweet."

She drove on past their house and dropped me off at mine. I thanked her and said goodbye to Jerome and got out of the car and forgot about them.

But two Saturday afternoons later Jerome rang the front doorbell again, his mother in the car, the motor running.

So all that fall and winter I went to every new movie at the Dolton Theater, free of charge, riding in the back-seat with Jerome while his mom talked on and on, usually about him, about some "mischief" he'd been up to lately, some prank he had pulled. You could tell she was trying to show me what a fun-loving person he was, what a fun friend he would make, but usually the mischievous prank he pulled seemed a lot more weird than fun-loving, like the time he dumped all the silverware into the fish tank.

"You boys are all alike," she cheerfully complained. "You're all a bunch of little rascals."

Jerome and I meanwhile sat there looking out our separate windows.

And after every movie, turning down our block, she would invite me over for brownies, or tollhouse cookies, or strawberry ice cream. And I would tell her my uncle Billy from Texas was visiting, or I had to help my brother with his homework, or get my mother some All-Bran for her constipation.

Between movies I never hung out with Jerome, or even saw him since we went to different grade schools, but every two or three weeks we went through the same routine, no matter what movie was showing. Sometimes it was something good, cowboys or cops or commandos, but I also remember seeing things like *Pillow Talk*, with Rock Hudson and Doris Day.

The best one I ever saw with Jerome, by far, also turned out to be the last one we saw together: *Rio Bravo*.

John Wayne was Sheriff John T. Chance, with a great-looking hat. Dean Martin was Dude, trying hard to stay off the bottle and be useful against the bad guys. Ricky Nelson was Colorado but really just Ricky Nelson in cowboy clothes. Walter Brennan was good old Stumpy, limping around and complaining in a high cranky voice. And Angie Dickinson, as Feathers, had this way of standing with her hands at her hips looking sideways at John Wayne, who she liked a lot.

After several setbacks they finally beat the bad guys, thanks in large part to Stumpy of all people. And it looked like Dude was going to lick his drinking problem after all. Ricky Nelson would be cheerfully moving on now. And John Wayne and Angie Dickinson were definitely going to be together, maybe get married, who knows? And as *The End* appeared on the screen, Dean Martin sang in his laid back way, "While the rolling Rio Bravo rolls along."

I felt great.

Leaving the theater with Jerome I just kept shaking my head: "That Stumpy. Who'd a thought? Y'know?"

Jerome shook his head. "Not me."

I liked Jerome. Jerome was all right, I decided. True, he didn't play any sports, and his clothes were far too neat and clean, and he wore a wristwatch, and probably had hobbies, and his name was *Jerome* . . .

When his mother asked me how was the movie I told her, "It was really good, Mrs. Fitzgerald." And when she asked Jerome he told her it was excellent.

"*Well*," she said, "listen to *you* two."

I knew what was coming next.

"Sounds to me like you fellas might enjoy a little *chin*-wag together, compare notes. Maybe over a nice bowl of tapioca. How does *that* sound?"

I was in such a good mood from the movie I told her that sounded fine.

She went quiet for a moment, driving along. Then she said, "Hear that, Jerome? We're having company."

"Ma?" he said.

"Yes, dear?"

"Can I talk to you?"

"Of course you can talk to me. What kind of—"

"In private?"

"Well, hon, that's a little difficult right now."

He laid the side of his head against the window.

"Jerome's a little nervous," she explained to me. "But he'll relax. Won't you, dear. Just give him a chance." She was looking at me in the rearview mirror. "Everyone deserves a chance. Don't you think?"

So I went to their house and ate tapioca from a red glass bowl at their kitchen table, sitting across from Jerome, his mom leaving us alone so we could talk to each other and become friends.

I told him the tapioca was good, the best I'd ever had, which was true. I told him my mom's was always gummy.

He said if I wanted seconds he was sorry but there wasn't any more.

I told him that was okay. I told him I was pretty full.

He nodded. He said I'd eaten an awful lot in the last couple of hours.

I gave a laugh, agreeing.

He started naming everything I'd eaten, ticking off each item on his fingers.

I corrected him about having two bags of popcorn, and took a final spoonful of tapioca.

"I hate you," he said quietly.

I looked at him.

He was sitting there with his hands in his lap, staring at me hard. "Get out of my house," he told me.

I set my spoon in the bowl and got up from the table.

He kept his eyes on me.

Stepping backwards I told him, "No problem. I was leaving anyway. My brother needs help with his homework—history, Columbus, fourteen ninety-two, all that."

He continued sitting there staring at me.

I turned around and got out of there.

THE INVASION OF THE BODY SNATCHERS

Near the very end of the movie the main character Miles shouts into the camera, wild-eyed, straight at me, *They're already here! You're next!*

Afterwards, across the dark between our beds, I asked Mike for his thoughts.

"I don't know . . ." he said. "Those pods . . ."

"What about 'em?"

"Seemed pretty goofy."

"What's goofy? The seeds came from outer space and grew into huge seed pods. How is that goofy?"

"With *aliens* inside?"

"*Growing* inside. They didn't just happen."

"And they come out looking exactly like different people in the town? How does *that* work?"

"*I* don't know, I'm not a scientist. Prob'ly had something to do with them being aliens."

"Yeah, well . . ."

"I mean, let's face it," I said.

"Face what?"

"Who knows?"

"Who knows what?"

"That's what I'm saying."

We were quiet for a moment.

"Well," he said, turning over the other way, "g'night."

"Sure that's a good idea?"

Going to sleep, I meant. That was when your alien double absorbed your mind.

He said if it happens it happens.

"It wouldn't bother you? Waking up as an alien?"

"Not if I *was* one."

That was true. When Miles' friend Jack comes back after turning into one, he's very peaceful—it's creepy—telling Miles and Becky in a smooth voice how silly it is to resist, how much better off they'll be if they just give up and go to sleep.

I asked Mike if he wanted to play some cards.

"Right now?"

"Some Old Maid. Nickel a hand. Whaddaya say."

"I'm tired."

"Couple hands, c'mon."

"Lemme sleep."

Mike was two years younger than me, but wasn't afraid of half the stuff I was. Sometimes it pissed me off.

"Tell you something," I said to him. "If you ever did turn into an alien, know what I would do?"

"Gut me like a catfish."

20

"That's right, pal."

We were quiet.

"I know what you're thinking," I told him.

"No, you don't."

"You're thinking, how would I know it wasn't you? How would I know it was really an alien *pretending* to be you? That's a real good question. And here's the answer. I would start noticing things. Little slip-ups."

"Yeah?" he said, half interested. "Like what."

"I don't know, you'd offer me a sip of your pop or something."

"Oh I don't share stuff?"

"Before I even asked."

We were quiet. I was losing him again. I went to the heart of the matter. "Or maybe you'd *really* slip up and start showing me a little respect."

He turned over this way again. "A little what?"

"You heard me."

"I don't show you enough respect?"

"Not really."

"Like how? Saluting you?"

"Make a joke."

"I'm asking."

"Skip it."

"I wanna hear."

"Drop it," I told him.

I didn't really want him to, but he did, he dropped it, and was quiet again. So I came out with it: "You think I'm a chicken, right? Don't you."

He didn't answer.

"Tell the truth."

I waited.

"I don't think you're a chicken," he finally said. "Just because you're afraid to go to sleep, that doesn't make you a—"

"Wait a minute, hold it, whoa. Just because I'm *what*?"

He didn't say anything.

"See, this is what I'm talking about. This is exactly what I'm talking about."

"What."

"Respect," I said.

"You're not afraid to go to sleep?"

"Oh, you mean because there's an alien out there in a giant seed pod waiting to take over my mind? Is that what you mean?"

"Well . . . yeah."

"Oh, my God. Listen carefully. It's a *movie*, Mike, okay? It's not real. Do you know the difference? I hope so. Otherwise, you know what? I hate to say it but you're insane."

"Hey, *I'm* not the one afraid of going to sleep. I *wanna* go to sleep."

"So *go* to sleep," I told him. "Who the hell's stoppin' ya?"

We were quiet. He turned over the other way again. He was going to sleep.

"Tell you the part of the movie *I* liked," I said. "Wanna hear?"

I waited.

"Mike?"

"What."

"Wanna hear the part *I* liked?"

"Go 'head."

"Becky," I said.

"Who?"

"The guy's girlfriend. She gave me a boner."

"I don't wanna hear."

"Thing was huge."

"G'night."

"Like a billy club."

We were quiet again.

I turned onto my back and lay staring up at the dark. After a minute I could feel him already asleep over there, part of the darkness now. I continued staring up at it, my heart beating hard. You wouldn't even know you were gone. That was the horrible thing about it. You wouldn't even know.

I turned onto my side again, towards Mike. I wanted to tell him I agreed with him about the pods. The pods were goofy. Ridiculous. *Funny* in fact, and I laughed out loud.

No response.

I laughed louder.

WEST SIDE STORY

I didn't know very much about my older sisters Cheryl and Linda, what made them tick. They were both good in school, I knew that, and were generally very nice to me. Sometimes they jitterbugged together, not smiling, bare-foot on the kitchen floor, Ricky Nelson or Fats Domino on their little suitcase-looking record player.

Cheryl had a boyfriend, Bob, who was tall and a little too handsome, played no baseball, and drove a car. I didn't like him. Linda had a colored picture of the singer Fabian taped to the wall above her bed. He had the kind of face you'd love to slap.

Sometimes one of them would send me to the drug-store with a little folded-up note for the cashier, which read, simply: *kotex*.

And I knew they liked the movie *West Side Story* because they took a train downtown to see it three times, and after-wards went around singing:

Tonight, tonight won't be just any night . . .
When you're a Jet you're a Jet all the way . . .
Maria, I just met a girl named Maria . . .

They had a big glossy book from the movie, full of colored stills, and I remember looking through it carefully, trying to get a fix on these two. There were pictures of hoody-looking teenagers in tight clothes dancing hard. The guys all looked like they had jack-knives on them and the girls all looked impure.

There were also pictures of a clean-looking couple, Tony and Maria, singing together, gazing into each other's eyes, apparently in love. The book said the movie was based on *Romeo and Juliet*, which I knew was a love story.

Love, love.

I studied one of the stills of Maria to see if I could imagine falling in love with her. She was in a white dress sitting on a fire escape singing down to me and I was down there singing up to her. We did that for a while. Then she sang for me to take my pants off, which I did, and she started singing like mad, and I went up there, singing.

But I knew that couldn't be what Cheryl and Linda had in mind when they sang, *Tonight, tonight won't be just any night . . .*

THE BIRDS

The summer it came to the Dolton Theater we had an actual outbreak of starling attacks in the neighborhood, nothing major at first, just now and then a starling or two swooping low over somebody's head on his way to the park. But from there it grew worse.

Skippy Whalen claimed a starling had actually lifted and carried away his ball cap.

Father Rowley was pointing in Brian Baumgartner's face outside the church, telling him what a lousy altar boy he was, when a starling dropped a load of milky poop on his finger and flew away laughing in that ugly voice of theirs.

According to the twins Jimmy and Joey, their feisty little dog Tuffy had fought off nine of them, killing one. For a nickel they would bring it out from their garage in a cardboard box and let you look. For a quarter you could have it.

There was also a story going around that a pack of them in Harvey, one town over, had actually carried off a little screaming baby right out of its stroller, right in front of the mother, who fainted dead away.

Kids were going around wearing football helmets in the middle of baseball season.

Nothing like this had ever happened before. No one could explain. It was like the starlings were inspired by the movie. But that seemed unlikely. This kid Andy Zahara had a theory. He said the movie had everyone afraid of birds, the starlings had somehow picked up on it, then counted how many of us versus them.

"They can count?"

"Sure they can."

"But what do they want?"

"To take over."

"Take over what?"

"Everything. They wanna run the place."

"Oh . . . my . . . God."

So far the sparrows were staying out of it, so were the robins, it was just the starlings—black, freckled, oily-looking things, tiny black buttons for eyes. I remember one evening in our alley I counted ten of them along a telephone wire squawking to each other:

—*There he is.*

—*Look at him.*

—*Little creep.*

—*Little coward.*

—*Let's crap in his hair.*

—*Let's pluck out his eyes.*

—*Ready?*

—*No, let's wait.*

—*Surprise him.*

They laughed and flew off together.

I blamed Alfred Hitchcock. Near the beginning of the movie I spotted him stepping out of a pet shop with two little dogs on a leash, heading down the sidewalk like he's got nothing to do with any of this. Snobby, coldblooded fatman—he probably *enjoyed* having golden-haired Tippy Hedron trapped in the attic with seagulls pecking her to shreds. That was how he got his kicks.

In the movie the people finally give up. Very carefully they get in the car and very slowly drive away from the farmhouse, letting the birds win. But we fought back. Anyway, some older kids did.

They put together a posse. A couple of them had BB-guns, others had rocks, bottles, baseball bats. I heard it got pretty ugly. Someone hit someone with a rock, the two of them started going at it, others joined in, and pretty soon everyone was shouting and punching and clubbing, the starlings watching from the trees, hugely amused.

This was the way we were spending our summer vacation. This was the way we were spending our three months of freedom.

By the time September came around, I didn't even mind that much.

Then sure enough, just like that, the starlings quit attacking people. In fact, they were hardly around anymore. They had ruined our summer and apparently that was all they'd had in mind.

CRYING AT MOVIES

Sitting at my desk in Sister Veronica Lawrence's class, staring out the window, I wondered what Alfred Hitchcock would come up with next. Maybe squirrels. I always felt like squirrels were just waiting for the chance.

SINGIN' IN THE RAIN

Dear Miss Reynolds,

I am writing to you in my pajamas on the front room couch with a lot of blankets and pillows because I have mono, which is called the kissing disease so I don't know how I got it, I have never kissed anyone, but I would like to kiss you. Guess what I just watched on The Early Show? Singing in the Rain. And I have to say, it was pretty sickening, especially your grinning boyfriend Gene Kelly, and that other guy, the little one who sang about making them laugh, he made me want to hit him with something. But I think you are very cute and spunky. May I call you Deb? I think I have a fever, Deb. I think I might be sicker than they think. In case you're wondering, I am thirteen, eighth grade, Sister Marie Alice's class, Queen of Apostles, Riverdale, suburb of Chicago, Illinois, United States, North America, planet Earth, the Universe. Sister Marie Alice is the smallest nun in the school but she can slap you so hard you see stars, like in a cartoon. Are you Catholic, Deb? Every time I think about you naked, do you know what I am doing? Driving the nails in deeper into His tender hands and feet. That's what Sister calls them, His tender hands and feet. I have the chills really bad, but I'm sweating like a pig—how can that be, Deb? Maybe I'm dying. If I died right now I would go straight to Hell and lay there twisting and screaming in pain, without any let-up, forever. Ever think about forever? It's hard to, then all of a sudden you get it and you think No! No! Right now though, all I'm thinking about is you, in a pair of yellow rain boots, and that's all, just the rain boots. Hope you don't mind. I'm trying to say I like you, Deb, a lot. I like the way you sing and the way you dance and I like that chubby face of yours. But I have to say, a couple of times during the movie I was sort of hating you. Know why? Because I could tell you knew what a cutie you were, singing and dancing away, laughing inside, knowing the way you were making me get.

Pray for me, Deb.

Sincerely,

Your number one fan

IT'S A WONDERFUL LIFE

It was on TV a few nights before Christmas, and although she didn't come out and say it, I think Mom wanted this to be a "family event," all of us watching it together, including Uncle Doug from the basement. She'd even made popcorn.

But Uncle Doug said he was going to stay down there and read. He was halfway through this huge book, *The Rise and Fall of the Third Reich*. He came up and took a bowl of popcorn, though.

So there was Mom and Dad and Nancy on the couch, Cheryl in one chair, Linda in the other, Mike and me on the floor. You could tell from the opening credits—the fancy handwriting trimmed with holly, the sleigh bells and jaunty violins—this was going to be long and corny and boring.

Cheryl lucked out, her boyfriend Bob coming to the back door just after the thing got started. She promised Mom and Dad she'd be back early.

"'Tell him to come in and watch the movie," Dad suggested.

Cheryl said quietly, "He seems upset."

"Oh, for Christ sake," Mom said.

Bob was a big handsome guy in collegiate-looking clothes but very sensitive and frequently upset.

So Cheryl got out of it. And then, while George in the movie was still a boy working at the town drugstore, the phone in the kitchen rang and Linda jumped up—"I got it!"—and ran out.

I heard her out there: "Hello?"

I waited.

"Oh my God," she said, "you're kidding. Hang on." She closed the kitchen door. It was her friend Mary Jo Foster, undoubtedly. "The Mouth," as Dad called her. Linda wouldn't be back.

Jimmy Stewart pretty soon took over in the movie as George the adult. He was talking to a pretty girl, Mary—Donna Reed from *The Donna Reed Show*—at a crowded dance. Then Dad started snoring, loud.

Mom woke him up. "We can't hear the *movie*."

"Just resting my eyes," he told her.

But by the time George and Mary were dancing the Charleston together he was snoring again.

"Jesus, Mary and Joseph," Mom said, and got him to his feet.

He walked off, holding up a large gnarly hand: "Goodnight."

"'Night, Dad," Mike and Nan and I told him.

After the dance George walked Mary home, telling her if she wanted the moon just say the word and he would throw a lasso around it. "I'd pull 'er down for ya, Mary."

Nancy said she was going to throw up and ran to the bathroom. I felt the same way, but she meant from eating too much buttered popcorn for a seven-year-old. Mom went to help her out—we were all bad at vomiting.

Which left me and Mike, lying on the floor, chins in our fists.

George and Mary went on talking together in the moonlight about their hopes and dreams and such.

Mike turned his head to the side, closed his eyes and went to sleep.

I could hear Mom in the bathroom coaching Nan, telling her to relax, just let it come up. Then Nan began making enormous sounds for a little kid. "That's it," Mom told her, "there you go, that's it . . ."

I turned the volume louder.

Mike woke up and went to bed.

I continued watching because no matter how bad a movie is, after I've stayed beyond a certain point I'm stuck with it.

By the time Mom got Nancy into bed and returned to the living room, George and Mary were ducking rice outside the church. Mom stood there looking around the room, shaking her head, muttering something.

"What?" I said.

"Nothing." She went around collecting popcorn bowls.

"Aren't you gonna watch?"

"I've seen it." She told me to turn the volume down and went to bed.

I felt bad for her. She'd had this nice idea.

About half an hour later George suddenly flipped out, right in front of the wife and kids on Christmas Eve, shouting and breaking things, like he couldn't stand being in this stupid sickening movie a minute longer, and ended up drunk on a bridge in the falling snow, about to jump.

This was more like it.

But then this little old sweet-faced angel named Clarence appears and shows George what a wonderful life he's actually had, and still has, and George goes running back to it, screaming *Merry Christmas* to everyone on the street, and at home he hugs his wife and children—*Oh, kids! Oh, Mary!*—then all the townspeople come over with an actual basket full of cash to save the building-and-loan company, and someone proposes a toast—*To George, the richest man in town*—meaning of course rich with family and friends who love him very much, and they all start singing, *Should auld acquaintance be forgot . . .*

Linda, finally off the phone, came in and stood there. "How is it?"

"Stinks to high heaven."

"Is that why you're crying?"

"I'm not crying."

She gave a little snort and walked out.

"I'm *not*."

ZORBA THE GREEK

I watched it with Nan. Afterwards I lay in bed staring up at the dark. Across the room Mike was asleep with the flu, now and then muttering stuff:

"That your bat?"

I wondered what Zorba would think of me.

He told Alan Bates, "A man needs madness," meaning you're too careful and scared to really live, *live*. Alan Bates knew Zorba was right. "Teach me to dance," he said, and Zorba got up from the log: "Dance? Did you say . . . *dance*?" Then that wonderful music, starting slow, as they danced together side by side on the white beach, an arm across each other's shoulder, Zorba chuckling deeply: "Boss, I have so much to tell you." And as the music grew faster they separated and danced backwards facing each other, arms wide, smiling in the sun, Alan Bates fully into it now, fully understanding, the camera receding until they were two tiny figures dancing like mad on the vast white beach, the music continuing faster, wilder, happier, the top of my head coming off. Then the credits.

Lying there now, staring up at the dark, I felt certain that if Zorba ever met me he would sadly shake his head. Take tonight, for example. What had I done with this precious gift of Life I'd been given? I watched a movie with my nine-year-old sister, both of us in our seersucker pajamas and house slippers.

"Throw it 'ere," Mike muttered.

I turned onto my side, facing the wall. "Books," Zorba said to Alan Bates, with scorn, "you only know books." I only knew movies.

There was a tap at the door.

"Yeah?"

Nan came in. "You awake?" she whispered.

I sat up and turned on the lamp. She was fully dressed. "What're you doing?" I said.

"Shhh." Our parents were asleep in the next room.

"Don't be shushing me, Nan."

"Some grounders now," Mike said.

She looked over at him.

"He's asleep," I explained.

"That's creepy." She looked at me. "Wanna go out?"

I didn't understand. "Out where?"

"To the park."

"What for?"

"Just . . . I don't know, go *out* there."

"Nan, it's eleven-thirty."

"Right," she said, nodding, meaning that was the idea.

I asked her point-blank, "This got something to do with the movie?"

She shrugged, embarrassed.

But she was right. *A man needs madness.*

I got up and pulled on my pants, right over my pajama bottoms—something Zorba would probably do in his haste to get out there and live, *live.*

"Bunt," Mike said.

We tiptoed into the living room, went out the front door and headed down the sidewalk towards the park a block away. It was a warm summer night with swarms of wet-looking stars, like in Greece. We walked without speaking past the silent houses to the end of the block, then crossed the street, entered the deeper darkness of the park and walked out into the middle of it.

Then we both just kind of stood there.

"So," I said. "Now what?"

She wasn't sure. "Feel like dancing around?"

"Not really. But go ahead," I told her.

"That's all right," she said.

We stood there looking around at the darkness, looking up at all those stars.

"Think there's anybody really like that?" she asked.

"Like Zorba, you mean?"

"Y'think?"

I was beginning to wonder. "I don't know, Nan. Maybe in Greece, somewhere like that."

"I liked him, didn't you?"

"Yeah, he was great."

"What if he was here right now," she said.

"That would be something," I agreed.

"What would we say to him?"

"We'd say, 'Hey, loved your movie.'"

"No, really."

"We'd say, 'Zorba? Will you teach us to dance?'"

"Right, and he'd say, 'Dance? Did you say . . . *dance*?'"

I began doing the Zorba theme, "*Dah*-duh, dah-dah," and so on, starting slow, Nan quietly joining in, both of us gradually speeding it up, louder and faster, louder and faster, neither of us dancing however, and after a minute we quit.

We stood there.

"Anyway . . ." I said.

"Great movie," she said.

"Wasn't it?" I said.

We headed back.

KING OF KINGS

It's on TV for the first time, on Good Friday, another Television Event, but there's only me on the floor and Mom and Dad on the couch behind me. Dad begins snoring by the first commercial, after the birth in the stable. Mom helps him up and they both say goodnight. I'm glad they're leaving. I can tell this movie is going to get to me.

Mary gets to me, with her sweet, Italian-looking face, and the way she gazes at her baby. The baby grows up to be Jeffrey Hunter, with a faraway look in his milky-blue eyes. And when he kneels in the water for John the Baptist he's got this tiny smile meaning *Yes, John, it's me*, with the Jesus theme music going.

Whenever they play it my eyes immediately fill with tears.

They spill over in the scene with the crippled kid curled up in bed, his limbs all twisted, the shadow of Jesus' outstretched hand on the wall, the kid sitting up, then standing precariously, amazement on his face, then stepping stiffly out of the room and into the light, the music rising while I lie there crying as quietly as I can.

By the time Jesus begins gathering His disciples I want to be gathered, too. I know the only thing that will ever make me truly happy is to follow Him, to live for Him alone, with that music playing. And when He teaches the multitude to pray, I whisper along:

". . . And lead us not into temptation but deliver us from evil, amen."

Then there's a scene in Herod's hall, with his step-daughter Salome. She looks a little older than me, maybe seventeen, milk-skinned, raven-haired, wearing heavy black eyeliner and a strange little smile.

"Dance for me," fat greasy Herod begs her. "Dance for me and I will give you anything you wish."

"Do you swear?"

"By my life, by my crown."

Slow snake-charmer music begins, with a hissing tambourine, and she rises from the cushions, barefooted, wearing a jewel in her bellybutton, a gold cobra headband, a gold bikini top and a skirt made of flimsy scarves. She stretches her long white arms, arching her back. Her stomach is so beautiful I want to cry out. Then, her head a little sadly to one side, she begins moving slowly, in a manner that makes me swallow repeatedly.

She gradually dances herself into a frenzy, the music keeping up as she whirls in front of Herod sitting on the floor, twirling her scarves in his woeful face.

That's how he looks. He looks woeful.

She finishes by sprawling on his throne, then slithering to the floor, where she tells him, out of breath: "I want . . . the head . . . of John . . . the Baptist."

He stares at her. "Have you gone mad? What can you want with the head of a man?"

She smiles that little smile of hers. "I want to look at it," she tells him.

Then a commercial.

I lie on my back staring up at the ceiling.

I feel sunk. I feel doomed. I would give *anything*, I realize. I would sell my soul without a moment's hesitation. I would follow her down to Hell. I don't care. She's all I want. She's all. I cover my eyes with my forearm and lie there quietly moaning.

"Are you all right?"

It's my mother.

I sit up. "I'm fine. Little stomach trouble. Too much Jello. Anyway, well, goodnight."

"I don't think Jello would—"

"Or something. I'm better now."

"There's some Pepto·Bismal—"

"I might try that."

"—in the medicine cabinet."

"Right. Thanks."

She goes back to bed.

The movie returns. John the Baptist kneels in his cell, head hung, weeping with joy as the blade is raised above his neck. I'm hoping for a scene with Salome receiving her reward, but the story moves on.

I don't give a shit about Jesus entering Jerusalem on a donkey, or about the Last Supper, Judas leaving early, or the torch-lit arrest in the Garden of Gethsemane, or His perfect silence before Pilate.

But then Pilate sends Him to Herod. And there she is again.

While Herod tries to make Him do tricks—cause thunder, turn a clay vase into gold—she's sitting on the floor in a corner of the screen dangling a little cage in front of her face, staring at a tiny bird in there. She looks so bored and unhappy. I want to crawl through the screen and up to her feet, along the cool marble floor, that strange little smile of hers on *my* face.

Herod sends Jesus back to Pilate and they finally crucify Him. Hanging there, He whispers, "It . . . is . . . finished."

I poke the Off button with my toe.

WHAT'S UP, TIGER LILY?

I was sitting alone at the kitchen table over my open geometry book, staring at the lines, the arcs, the angles, and that odd little thing called pi, when the phone on the countertop began ringing. It was never for me, so I let it.

Mom called out from *Hawaii Five-O* in the front room, "Will someone *get* that?"

Dad was in bed already, Nancy in her room with an art project, Mike still at his basketball game, Cheryl and Linda both married, Uncle Doug in his own apartment now, so I got it. "Hello?" I sat on the stool.

Someone seemed to be crying, hard. It sounded like Linda.

I stood up. "Lin? What's the matter? Hey, Ma!" I told Linda to hold on, I was getting Mom. But she wasn't crying, she was laughing. "Turn on channel five!" she said, and got off. I hung up and hurried towards the front room, passing Mom on the way.

"What the hell's going on?" she said, following me back in. "What're you doing? Who was it?"

"Lin. She said turn on five."

"I'm in the middle of—"

"She said it's important."

"A storm?"

"Could be." I turned to channel five.

Nan came in, holding a magic marker, and the three of us stood there watching a Japanese-looking man in a necktie driving a car with a very pretty Japanese-looking woman beside him.

—*You want egg salad? I'll give you egg salad*, he said, the words unrelated to the movements of his mouth. *Did you bring the mayonnaise?*

—*Mayonnaise?* the woman said.

—*I told you to take a jar!*

"Is this the right channel?" Mom asked.

"She said five, this is five."

—*Oh, never mind*, said the man. *We can always use Miracle Whip.*

Nan was chuckling. "What *is* this?"

I shook my head. "Lin said turn it on."

Mom sighed. "She's losing it."

We watched some more. Evidently someone had taken a Japanese James Bond-type movie and dubbed in their own goofy story, about the search for a secret recipe for the world's greatest egg salad. Some of it was pretty funny and Nan and I were laughing, but Mom kept shaking her head and clicking her tongue at the silliness of it and finally with a large sigh said she was going to bed.

We told her goodnight.

After a while the humor got pretty lame:

—*Wong's desperate for that recipe.*

—*Why?*

—*He's an egg salad addict.*

—*You mean he's hooked on it?*

—*He's got a chicken on his back.*

Nan eventually returned to her scissors and paste and construction paper, but I sat on the couch and watched the rest of it, the alternative being geometry.

It ended with a Pan Am jet taking off while we hear the voice of the hero, who's decided he's a Pan Am jet: *I'm almost to the end of the runway, rum-rum-rum, here I go, up into the air . . .*

I was settling back down at the kitchen table, when the phone rang again. It was Linda, apologizing. She said the movie was so funny before she called.

I forgave her.

"The guy who talked like Peter Lorre was funny," she said. "Didn't you think?"

"He was all right."

"Did you see him with the chicken?"

"That wasn't bad."

"I nearly peed."

"Listen, how do you get the circumference of a circle?"

"Oh, God. Let me think . . ."

"I hate this stuff."

"Pi times the radius squared," she said.

"Okay, what *is* that thing."

"What thing."

"Pi. What *is* that."

"You don't know?"

"I know what it *looks* like."

She laughed.

"I got a *test* tomorrow, Lin."

"All right, don't have a conniption." She tried explaining pi to me, carefully. "Okay?" she said when she was finally through.

"Got it," I told her. "Thanks."

I was back at the table staring at that same page, thinking about Japanese women, their long black hair, their long white arms. Then Mike walked in, carrying his duffel bag, looking sad and tired.

"You lose?"

He nodded, on his way to the refrigerator. "Big time."

I asked him how *he* did.

"Shitty." He stood leaning against the open refrigerator door, staring in.

"You missed a really funny movie," I told him.

"Yeah?" He took a hit from a carton of orange juice.

"Wanna hear about it?"

"Nah." He took another hit.

"C'mon, it's really funny. Cheer you up."

He put the carton back. "That's okay," he said, and swung the door shut.

"It was Japanese," I said, "but get this, someone dubbed in a totally different movie, a totally different story. What a riot."

He leaned his back against the refrigerator. "How do you know it was different?"

"How do I . . . well, for one thing, it was all about egg salad, okay? I don't think the original was about *egg* salad."

"How do you know?"

I nodded. "Okay, you're being like this because you lost your game, which is fine, I understand, but I've got a test tomorrow, Mike, okay? So, if you don't mind . . ."

"Tell me the movie."

"That's all right."

"Go ahead."

"I don't need your pity."

He sighed, and headed for bed.

"You wouldn't happen to know anything about pi, would you?"

He turned. "How do you mean?"

"In geometry," I explained. "You haven't had it, I know. I just thought . . ."

"Call Linda. She'll know."

"Good idea."

He went to bed.

I sat there. I looked down at that same page. I got up and called Cheryl.

She tried hard to remember pi but she couldn't, not in a way that helped. "Lin would know," she said.

"I already talked to her. She explained it very carefully and I still didn't get it. I'm too dumb. I should just drop out of school, you know?"

"John . . ."

"Just drop out of *life*," I added. This was a weakness I sometimes had when talking to Cheryl—saying things like that, getting her to mother me. "Let's face it," I said, "I'm a loser."

Cheryl came through with a wonderful, motherly pep talk, calling me "hon," bringing tears to my eyes, and afterwards I sat back down at the table feeling appreciated, worthy and loved, though still in the dark regarding pi.

I decided what I needed was a bowl of Frosted Flakes. *Then* we'd get to the bottom of this pi business.

But we were all out. The box was there, but it was empty. Someone had eaten the last of it and then, instead of throwing out the box, had put it back in the cupboard to make a fool out of me.

I went to Nan's room. Her light was still on. I opened the door and stood there holding the box. "Who did this? Do you know?"

She was kneeling on the floor over a poster board, surrounded by scraps of colored construction paper. "Did what."

"This," I said, shaking the empty box.

"Who finished it, you mean?"

"Finished it and then . . ."

She waited.

I shook my head. "Never mind." I didn't really care. I nodded at her project. "What's this for?"

"Sister Michael Denise."

Pasted to the board were plump white clouds, assorted birds, trees, mossy rocks, tall grass, wildflowers, very large mushrooms, and these intensely happy-looking little bug-like people, or people-like bugs, some of them playing musical instruments, one of them waving to the viewer.

I laughed.

"Pretty dumb?" she asked.

I came in and sat on the edge of her bed and looked at it some more. "I like it," I told her, nodding. I wanted to live there, sitting on a mushroom, playing the banjo.

"How'd the movie end?" she asked.

"He thinks he's an airplane."

"Oh, dear," she said, sounding like Gram.

I watched her carefully paste a tiny yellow bird to the lower branch of a tree. Then she sat back on her heels and considered the whole scene.

"Done," I told her. "Leave it."

"Not too creepy?"

"What's creepy?"

"The way they're smiling."

"They're *happy*. What's wrong with that?"

"They look like they're on medication."

"Just *leave* it, Nan, will ya?" I got up with my empty cereal box and trudged to the door.

"What's the matter?"

"Nothing. I don't suppose you know anything about pi."

"I know I *like* pie."

"What's your favorite?"

"Pumpkin."

"That's a good one."

"What about you?"

"I don't know. Apple, I guess."

She nodded.

I told her goodnight and went to bed. What the hell, it wouldn't be the first test I ever flunked.

HAMLET

My senior year in high school I was depressed a lot and hated everything, everything was sickening, so when I read, with difficulty, Shakespeare's *Hamlet* for Miss Giancola's English class I was pleased to see how depressed and disgusted the main character was, how suicidal even:

"To be or not to be . . ."

Miss Giancola told us Hamlet was "melancholy," a new word, meaning unhappy in a deep, thoughtful way.

I started going around thinking of myself as melancholy, thinking of myself as Hamlet: *How weary, stale, flat and unprofitable seem to me all the uses of this world*, I would reflect on my way to gym class, or in lunch line with my tray, or staring out the bus window. *Fie upon it, fie.*

Miss Giancola said Prince Hamlet was a tormented young man, torn between thought and action.

I knew *that* feeling.

She said he was a tragic hero.

Exactly.

Then, over one Thursday and Friday, she set up a screen in front of the room, a projector in the back, and showed us the movie version, starring Laurence Olivier.

It was old, in black and white, with a lot of large gloomy shadows, and that seemed right, but I didn't like Laurence Olivier, not at all. He had plenty of melancholy, tons of it, but there was something smug about him, as if being melancholy made him better than everyone. Even when he was calling himself names—a rogue, a drab, an ass, a scullion—it only added to his smugness, for after all, who in the entire castle, who in all of *Denmark*, would be half so hard on himself? Plus, he dressed like a ballet dancer.

He was sickening and I hated him.

The one person in the movie who seemed to be in real pain was the murderous king, especially when he tries to pray for forgiveness, but knows he's not really sorry. "Oh wretched state, oh bosom black as death!" he cries, without a trace of pleasure.

"To be," Laurence Olivier whispers with a lofty look on his smooth face, near the edge of a high cliff, "or not to be." But even if you haven't read the play, you know he's not going to jump.

At the end of the movie, everyone is dead but Horatio, Miss Giancola turned the lights back on and gave us an assignment for the weekend: two hundred words, *Why Hamlet Procrastinates*. Then the bell, and we left the room.

I headed down the loud crowded hallway towards the gym. *How weary, stale, flat and unprofitable*, I began to myself, but then I quit. It wasn't working. I felt more like Laurence Olivier than Hamlet. And I hated Laurence Olivier. Hated gym class, hated school, hated everything.

ELVIRA MADIGAN

The first time I ever had sex was early in my freshman year at college, with an aggressive little freckle-faced girl named Melissa, who helped me out of my clothes in the storage room of the student-center cafeteria where we bussed tables together three evenings a week. "Don't be nervous," she told me.

It was all over in a minute, possibly less. But I fell in love.

After that one time, though, Melissa wouldn't have sex with me anymore. I was too much like a rabbit. That was how she put it. "Sorry, you're too much like a rabbit." I had never seen rabbits having sex, but I could imagine them: quick and feverish and comical-looking.

Seeing her at work became very painful, the way she looked—God, so cute—in her starched white coat, the sleeves down around her knuckles, and the way she ignored me:

Sorry, you're too much like a rabbit.

I needed some kind of instruction. But where could I possibly go? I felt so desperate I ended up talking to my roommate one night, deliberately turning in when he did so I could speak across the dark between our beds.

"Hey, Greg?"

"What."

I hesitated. "Listen . . ."

"Yeah?"

"Can I ask you something?"

"Go ahead."

I went ahead: "How do you have sex with a woman so that *she* enjoys it too?"

He said quietly, "Jesus," turning over the other way.

I always felt like he considered me a rather creepy guy and now I had surely confirmed it. He had a girlfriend Kathy, a set of buddies, an electric Coors sign on his wall along with a poster of W.C. Fields in a top hat playing cards. I didn't even have a poster. I had thought about getting one, but I felt a poster ought to say something about yourself, and what could I possibly say?

Then I saw in the school paper, there was this movie in town at the Egyptian Theater, a love story from Sweden, which might be instructive.

The Egyptian Theater was very old, with a large heavy curtain in front of the screen, a high ceiling studded with tiny stars, and way up there along the walls these life-sized Egyptian figures, each one lit from its pedestal with a spooky blue light.

Sitting there waiting for the curtain to open, I felt some deep mystery was about to be revealed.

Turned out, there wasn't any actual sex in the movie at all. It was definitely a love story, and Swedish—you had to read what they were saying—but they never even took their clothes off.

Even so, I was glad I went.

It was about this young cavalry officer who deserts the army to run off with a beautiful circus tightrope-walker, and they're so in love it's like they're in another world, running around a sunny field in slow-motion, chasing little white butterflies, for example, laughing like they can hardly believe how happy they are, this beautiful dreamy Mozart music meanwhile playing.

"I barely recognize myself," he says to her at one point.

"Now I know who I am," she says to him.

But meanwhile the real world is still out there, brutal and stupid, and closing in.

So they kill themselves.

They go on a picnic and in their basket bring hardboiled eggs, bread, wine, cheese and a pistol. He tries to shoot her while they're hugging under a tree but he can't do it, so she gets up and goes wandering around the field. We see him aiming the pistol. Then we see her about to cup a butterfly in her palms. There's a gunshot and the frame freezes. She still has a tiny smile on her face. There's another gunshot and the screen goes black.

I sat there, letting everyone leave. Then I got up slowly.

I went wandering around, up and down side streets. It

was a warm October night, with a moon, and as I walked I thought about the soldier and the circus girl, about Melissa, about love, oh love . . .

I ended up at the lagoon, under a tree. There was no one around, just some ducks muttering in the weeds on the other side. I sat there, that dreamy theme music still playing in my head. Now and then the silhouette of a duck would come gliding, stately, through the wiggling line of moonlight on the water.

God, I thought. If only Melissa were here right now. I would not be like a rabbit. I would kiss her eyelids, carefully, one and then the other, cupping her face in my hands.

THE GRADUATE

As soon as we stepped from the theater into the lobby, Marcia said she had to use the ladies room and walked off. I waited, leaning against the wall, smoking a Salem.

"Enjoy your popcorn?" a guy asked me, walking by, and his girlfriend threw back her head and laughed.

I didn't understand.

Then I noticed the front of my sweater. It was covered with popcorn—it was made of popcorn. There were whole kernels, fragments, even some seeds in there. I began frantically brushing and picking and pulling them off, finishing just in time.

"Go for some coffee?" I asked Marcia, leaning against the wall once again, smoking a Salem.

Marcia was my roommate Eric's girlfriend's roommate. I'd only met her once, just for a minute, but the next day she actually called me up and asked me out, which bewildered me because she was tall, a senior, an English major, on the pretty side, and I was short, a sophomore, Unde-cided, on the homely side. But I told her, "Yeah. Sure. You bet."

The movie was her idea.

Afterwards we went for coffee at the student center, sit-ting across from each other in a booth, sharing an ashtray. Turned out, this was her third time seeing the movie. I thought parts of it were funny and it was pretty exciting towards the end, but Marcia *loved* the movie—her word—especially Dustin Hoffman.

"You mean . . . as an actor?"

"I mean Ben," she said. "Benjamin."

That was the guy Dustin Hoffman played.

"You love Benjamin?"

She sipped her coffee.

She loved Benjamin.

Once again I was bewildered. First of all, Benjamin was short and looked like a rodent. Plus, he was this very depressed, very *depressing* guy. I considered it a major flaw in the movie to have someone as beautiful as Elaine be interested in a guy like Benjamin. It just didn't seem believable. I could see her with Steve McQueen, someone like that. But Dustin Hoffman. Even his voice was wimpy. Whiny, in fact.

I asked Marcia, right up front, what she found so attrac-tive about Dustin Hoffman—or Benjamin—either one.

"He's very sad, very sensitive, very sweet," she said, just like that.

I told her I thought he was very annoying.

"Annoying?" she said, her hackles up.

"Moping around, staring at his goldfish . . ."

She sat there shaking her head, just sat there looking at me and shaking her head.

"What," I said.

She tried to explain why Benjamin was so unhappy. It was because he was spiritually unfulfilled. He had all these achievements and material things, everything society says is *supposed* to make you happy, but he felt totally empty inside. She said that was such a great moment in the movie when his expensive little sports car runs out of gas, the symbolism of it.

I said, "You can tell you're an English major."

She lifted her chin. "What's wrong with that?"

"Nothing. I'm just saying."

She sighed, like it was hopeless even talking to me, and sipped her coffee.

I sipped mine.

This wasn't working out.

She didn't like me very much, that was the problem. And I didn't like *her* a hell of a lot either, come to that. But she was definitely on the pretty side and she wasn't even wearing any make-up. I wanted her to like me so we could go out again and possibly eventually have sex together and then our different tastes in movies wouldn't matter so much.

"Marcia?"

"What."

"Would you like a muffin?"

"You know what's so ironic?" she said, giving a little ironic laugh. "I wanted to go out with you because you look like Dustin Hoffman and I thought *maybe*—"

"Wait a minute, hold it."

"What."

"You think I look like Dustin *Hoff*man?"

"Well, you're short, and you have a big nose, and you're kind of sad-looking, and I thought maybe you'd be like Benjamin." She shook her head and said, "Boy," meaning boy was she ever wrong about *that*.

We sat there.

I told her *I* could get pretty sad sometimes. "*Damn* sad, as a matter of fact."

"Right," she said, looking off, smoking.

I told her the popcorn-on-my-sweater story, how that girl had thrown back her head and laughed at me standing there all sad and covered with popcorn.

It didn't move her at all. She wanted to know how I could have gotten that much popcorn on my sweater—did I have trouble finding my mouth in the dark?

We finished our coffee and I walked her home.

I said goodnight outside the front door of her building and didn't even bother asking for another date. I just turned and walked off, with my head hung, hands deep in my pockets, dragging my feet . . .

"Wait," Marcia said.

I almost burst out laughing. I almost blew it.

LA DOLCE VITA

I agreed with Marcia about Fellini using water as a unifying metaphor, especially in the fountain scene. "The Fountain of Life, right?"

"Very good," she said, lying naked beside me, sharing a Salem.

"He's there with her," I went on, "*in* the fountain, water falling all around . . ."

"So baptismal," she observed.

"Very much so," I agreed. "Yes."

We belonged to the University Foreign Film Society, which featured a discussion each week after the movie, but we never stayed for it, preferring to return to her apartment for sex, afterwards discussing the movie ourselves. So far we'd seen Bergman's *Seventh Seal*, which we both considered completely brilliant; Truffaut's *Breathless*, which I thought was completely brilliant, but Marcia regarded as somewhat flawed; Kurosawa's *Stray Dog*, which we agreed was excellent, but not quite brilliant; and tonight's *La Dolce Vita*, which we hadn't decided on yet.

"But then, what happens next?" she said. "Remember?"

"I'm trying to think . . ."

"Suddenly . . . ?"

"He kisses her?"

"The water, what happens to the water."

"Right, it's turned *off*. The fountain goes dry. They're just standing there."

"Modern man," she said, "in a spiritual drought."

"Bingo."

She lit another cigarette.

I said something about Anita Ekberg having remarkably large breasts.

"That's real insightful."

"No, I'm *saying*, they were probably, you know . . ."

"Fake?"

"Symbolic."

"Of what?"

"*I* don't know . . . the milk of human kindness?"

She laughed, getting up. "I gotta pee."

I lay there smoking, staring up at a complicated network of cracks in the ceiling. During the movie I felt sure they would eventually show Anita Ekberg's entire tits, this being an Italian movie, but they never did. Marcia's tits were tiny but I liked them and in fact I liked her entire long scrawny body quite a lot. Sometimes during sex I felt like we must be in love, or very nearly, the heated way we carried on and the things we said, looking each other dead in the eye, like lovers in a European movie—*film*, I mean. She was always correcting me about that: America made movies, Europe made films.

When she came back from the bathroom we talked some more about *La Dolce Vita* and the various ways Fellini showed modern man in a spiritual drought, and decided the film was completely brilliant, and had some more sex.

Afterwards she lit another cigarette. I waited for her to pass it to me but she didn't. She lay there staring up at the ceiling and told me she wished to be alone.

"What's the matter?"

She didn't answer.

"What'd I do?"

"Please just go."

"*Tell* me. What'd I do?"

"Please? Just go?"

I didn't understand. I thought I'd performed pretty well, sexually and conversationally. But this was her apartment, so I got up and started pulling on my clothes.

"What are you doing?" she said, sitting up.

"You told me to go. So I'm going."

"Just like that?"

I shrugged. "It's your apartment."

"You could at least pretend to be hurt."

"I *am* hurt. I don't have to pretend."

"Well? So?"

I looked at her.

She seemed to be waiting.

I told her, "I don't understand. What do you want me to do?"

"*Some*thing, for God sakes."

It occurred to me what she wanted. She wanted a scene. I did my best. Turning up my palms I said to her, "I mean, you just tell me to *go*? Like I'm some kind of a . . ."

"Go ahead. Say it," she told me, stabbing out her cigarette in the ash tray. "You've been wanting to. Let's hear it. Let's have it allll out."

"Like I'm some kind of a . . ." I needed a script. "Some kind of a . . ."

"Oh, forget it," she said, and lay back down.

"Fine," I told her, "gladly," and resumed getting dressed.

She sat up again. "Wait, John. Please don't go? I'm so afraid." She really looked it too.

"Afraid of what," I asked her.

She lay back again, staring at the ceiling. "Of Nothing," she said. "The great . . . vast . . . endless . . . absolute . . . Nothing."

I sat on the edge of the bed. "Yes," I said to her, deepening my voice a little. "I know what you mean."

"Hold me, John? Please hold me?"

I reached down and pulled her bony body up into my arms.

"Oh, God," she said, "life is so devoid of meaning."

"I know," I said. "It's like we're in some kind of a . . . I don't know, some kind of spiritual *drought*."

She started shaking and I held her tight and said her

68

name because I thought she was crying, but she wasn't, she was laughing. "I'm sorry," she said, unable to stop.

I let go of her, got up and once again resumed getting dressed. "I don't need this bullshit, Marcia," I told her, buttoning my shirt. "You know? I really and truly don't need this."

"Oh, is that right," she said, sitting up again. "So what *do* you need, John? Can you tell me? Do you even know? I'm serious. *Do* you?"

"Well . . . I guess that pretty much depends on what you mean by 'need.' On the one hand—"

"Oh, go away," she told me with disgust, throwing herself down again, this time rolling over to face the wall.

I looked at her there, all curled up, showing the bones of her spine. "Marcia, I don't understand. What's the matter? Honest to God, I don't even know anymore if you're—"

"Stop torturing me!" she cried, curling up even more.

I stood there, dressed now. I didn't want to leave her like this, in a state, even a mostly cinematic one. But she was wearing me out. I sat on the edge of the bed, my back to her.

"Marcia?"

I waited.

"What," she finally said.

"Want to go get something to eat?"

"It's too late, John. Don't you understand? It's too late."

"The Junction's open till midnight."

"I hate that place."

"All right, fine," I said, giving up. I told her goodnight and started to leave.

"Oh, for God sakes," she said, rolling away from the wall. "If you're gonna go pout . . ."

I waited while she got dressed.

EASY RIDER

"Okay, you know what?" Jeremy said, walking with me away from the Egyptian Theater. "That, without a doubt, was the most boring movie I have ever—no, I'll go further—that was the most boring two *hours* I have ever spent in my entire fucking life."

I had talked him into seeing it. I thought it might be good for him.

"You owe me two hours of my life, pal," he said.

He was a very overweight marketing major in a camel's hair coat and earmuffs, and I was a skinny hippie in a pony tail and pancho. We shared a little apartment in town. His ad for a roommate had stated flat-out, *No longhairs*, but the semester was starting by the time I came by and he was desperate.

"You shoulda got high first," I told him as we walked along. "You shoulda smoked up." I was always trying to get him to smoke a little pot, at least try it. I had this notion it would cure him of being a marketing major.

He asked me, "What's that say about a movie, you have to be drugged to enjoy it, what's that say?"

"I just think it woulda come across better, that's all."

"If I was fucked up?"

"In a more . . . expansive state."

"Fucked up."

We headed down a quiet side street.

"Wasn't even a story, for Christ sake," he muttered.

"It's not that kind of movie," I told him.

"What kinda movie doesn't have a story?"

"It's more like a . . . like a mythic journey," I explained.

"Oh please. Two jag-offs riding around on motorcycles, that's the whole fuckin' movie."

"What about Jack Nicholson," I reminded him.

He nodded, agreeing.

"Pretty funny?" I said.

"I will admit."

"How 'bout where he's riding on the back of—"

"Right, in his fuckin' *football* helmet—"

"Grinning like an idiot—"

"Waving a rubber *pork* chop."

We laughed.

"See?" I said.

"What."

"You enjoyed it."

"The Jack Nicholson part. Fifteen minutes."

"It was more than fifteen—"

"Check it out," he said quickly, a pretty girl approaching. When she got near enough he started telling me off:

"Oh yeah? Is that right. Well, let me tell you something, you silly son of a bitch, and you listen good, you understand? You listen real, *real* good."

She hurried by without glancing at either of us.

He turned around and walked backwards a few steps, speaking low: "Oh, yeah . . . oh, yeah."

Jeremy didn't have a girlfriend and in fact I had a pretty good hunch he'd never been laid.

Turning frontwards again he said, "Very choice. Very choice indeed."

I wanted to get back to the movie. It bothered me that he thought it stank. "That was pretty awful, wasn't it? Jack Nicholson getting killed like that? By those rednecks? In his *sleeping* bag?"

"That was shitty," he agreed. "Mostly because now it was back to just Peter Fonda and what's-his-face."

"Dennis Hopper."

"Now *there's* a great actor: 'Wow, man, that's really weird, man, really far out, man.'" He looked at me. "*You're* a fuckin' English major, you call that good dialogue?"

During the movie it had in fact occurred to me that Dennis Hopper was using the word "man" a lot more than he probably needed to.

We turned down another side street, towards the apartment a couple blocks away. "What about the ending?" I asked. "Any thoughts on that?"

"I liked the ending very much. Know why?"

"Because it was over?"

"There ya go."

"You're telling me you didn't feel bad, at all?"

"About *those* two bozos?"

"I found it very disturbing."

"*You're* fucking very disturbing."

"I don't mean about just them," I said.

"Oh, right, let me guess, it *symbolized* something, right? The end of the whole entire—"

"Remember where Peter Fonda says, 'We blew it'? Near the end of the movie? Remember? They're passing a joint back and forth—"

"Yeah, *that* narrows it down."

"And he says to Dennis Hopper, 'We blew it.' He doesn't explain. He just says, 'We blew it.' Remember?"

"Right, he's talking about the movie. He's saying we tried to make a good movie but we fuckin' blew it."

"What he's *saying*," I explained, "he's saying we lost our way. All of us. We didn't make it to the top of the mountain. We got pretty far, it was a real good try, a noble try, but somehow, somewhere, we lost our way. We blew it."

We were quiet for a few steps.

Then he said, in the Tin Man's sappy voice, "'Now I *know* I've got a heart, because it's breaking.'"

"Fuck you, Jeremy."

He just smiled at me, sadly, shaking his big head. "You dumb shit. *God* you're dumb. It's the end of the fuckin' road all right, know why? Wanna know why?"

"Listening."

"Because the minute they start making *movies* out of something, forget it, it's over. Next thing? *We* move in."

I looked at him. "How do you mean?"

"Listen, if I was *with* somebody now? Say like Pepsi? Know what I'd be doing? Hippie ads. Rock music, strobe lights, flower children sucking down our product like they're getting stoned on it." He took an imaginary swig, with glugging sounds, then gave a long blissful sigh: "Wow, man," he drawled. "Pepsi, man." Then, in my face: "Gets me hiiiigh."

I stopped walking.

He laughed, spread his arms and went circling down the sidewalk, gazing up at the starry sky, chanting, "Pepsicola . . . Pepsicola . . ."

I stood there hating him.

THE SPIRIT OF THE BEEHIVE

After college I was living in Chicago on the near northside in a little studio apartment with mice in the walls. At night I could hear them scurrying around in there, trying to find a way in.

I wrote a poem about them but it stank. Back then I was writing poems about everything and they all stank and I knew it but I kept trying anyway. I don't know why.

My sister Nan used to come by on Saturday mornings, with a plant or a basket of potpourri, something to cheer the place up a little. I was usually still in my pajamas, empty beer cans and overloaded ashtrays and crumpled papers and dirty socks lying around, which would have been appropriate if the poems were any good, but they weren't, so it wasn't a poet's hovel, it was just a messy, depressing little apartment.

Nevertheless I would often go ahead and show poor Nan my latest poem. She would sit on the edge of the unmade bed, still in her coat, and read it carefully. Then she would look up at me, nodding, nodding: "This is really good."

"Yeah, right."

"No, really."

I'd snatch it back.

"You should send it somewhere," she would tell me.

I'd crumple it up and send it across the room.

"I *like* it, John."

"Let's get outa here."

We'd take a bus to the Loop and go wandering around, yakking away, laughing a lot. Nancy has always been able to make me laugh, no matter how miserable I've made up my mind to be.

Sometimes we would go somewhere, a donut shop or a gallery. I remember one time it started raining and we went into the furniture department at Marshall Fields and continued our conversation from a pair of comfortable matching lounge chairs. Some guy in a tie eventually came over and told us we had to leave. I jumped up and spread my arms. "Why? What are we doing? Can you tell me? We're just sitting here." Nan got me out of there. It wasn't raining anymore and we headed down to the lake to look at the therapeutic waves, the gulls, a tanker out on the horizon.

One Saturday we ended up seeing a very strange beautiful movie at the Art Institute, called *The Spirit of the Beehive*. It was from Spain, with subtitles, about a little girl named Isabella. That's all I remember about it now, except that Isabella had large dark eyes, her father kept bees, and at one point she stood on her tiptoes to look down a very deep well.

I also remember the movie left a powerful impression on both of us, and afterwards we hurried across Michigan Avenue and sat in a booth in The Gallery restaurant over coffee trying to put it all together. We had trouble. We considered the title. True, her father kept bees, but so what?

We decided the movie was basically about life being indeed a mystery, a deep dark mystery.

"Like that well she looks down," I said.

Nan pointed at me, nodding: "Right."

Good enough. We ordered some pie.

Afterwards we split the check and went out into the slanting, late-afternoon light, people hurrying by, north and south. We stood out of the way, deciding which direction. Not that it mattered. Life was a mystery. We headed north. As we walked along, I felt another poem coming.

WUTHERING HEIGHTS

Uncle Doug called me up one Sunday afternoon out of the blue wanting to know if I'd ever seen a movie called *Withering Heights*. He meant "wuthering," but it was Uncle Doug, so I didn't correct him. I told him yes I'd seen it, more than once in fact.

"So you *like* the movie. That what you're saying?"

"Well . . . how do *you* feel about it?" I asked.

"Never mind that. I'm asking *you*. Your aunt Ro and I just watched it on TV and she thinks it's a great movie, she thinks it's absolutely fantastic, and I know you like a lot of that English stuff, so we wanted *your* opinion. So: great movie or not?"

I was pretty certain "not" was the right answer, but here was timid Aunt Ro apparently standing up to him for once and I wanted to be supportive, as far as I could.

"It's a very well-*made* movie," I said to him. "It's definitely very well made."

"All right. I'll give you that. What else? Anything else?"

"Got some great performances."

"Laurence Olivier, all that, sure, you bet. But here's the question, John. All things being equal, putting all that aside, is it a great movie? In your opinion? Yes or no."

"Is that the word she used? 'Great'?"

"Hang on." He spoke to Aunt Ro: "You're saying it's a *great* movie, right? That's the word you want? 'Great'? She's nodding her head. She's sitting there nodding her head with this stubborn look on her face."

I heard in the background, "I don't think I'm being—"

"Do you mind? I'm trying to talk to my nephew. Go ahead," he told me.

"He's my nephew too," I heard.

"I'm tryna *talk* here, will ya? Jesus."

"Uncle Doug . . ."

"Yeah, go ahead, John. Sorry about that."

"I don't think . . ." I hesitated.

"What. You don't think what."

I went ahead: "I don't think you should yell at her like that."

He was quiet for a moment. Then he said, "John doesn't think I should yell at you like that."

"Thank you, John," she called out.

"Did you hear that?"

"Tell her she's welcome."

"He says you're welcome. You oughta see her, John. She's sitting there with a little smirk on her face now, thanks to you."

"Huh."

"No, I'll tell you something, she's a remarkable woman, your aunt Ro. She's quite a remarkable—"

"Oh, stop it," I heard her say.

"I'm talking to John!" he yelled. "I'm telling *John*, do you mind?"

I didn't hear a reply.

"Telling me to stop," he muttered. "Go ahead, John. You were saying."

"I don't . . . think I was, was I?"

"I don't know. I'm all confused now. *See?*" he said to her. "How you got me? Are you happy now?"

"No," I heard her say.

"Anyway, here's my point, John. It's a great movie for women—your aunt Ro's the proof, you shoulda seen the tears, *buckets*, I'm not kidding—but see, being a great movie for women doesn't make it a great movie, not by a long shot. That's all I was trying to tell her, but she wouldn't listen. 'Call your nephew John,' she says. 'I'll bet *he* thinks it's a great movie.' And I said to her, 'The hell he will.' You know why? You know what I was thinking about, don't you? All those war movies you and I used to watch. Remember?"

"With John Wayne," I said, "yeah."

"That's it. There you go. You still like those? Now that you been to college and all that? You still appreciate those?"

"Absolutely," I told him.

"Attaboy." Then, to Aunt Ro: "He says he prefers John Wayne movies."

"Uncle Doug?" I said.

"Yeah?"

"I didn't say I pre*fer*—"

"But here's my point, John, if you'll let me finish."

"Sorry."

"There's movies for women and there's movies for men, that's all I'm saying. There's movies like *Back to Bataan*, or *Pork Chop Hill*, or—"

"*Sands of Iwo Jima*," I threw in.

"There you go. Exactly. You get my point. There's movies like that and then there's, you know, shit like this."

"It's not shit, Uncle Doug," I said to him. "I don't think it's shit."

"Hey, watch the mouth."

"Sorry."

"So you're taking *her* side? Is that it?"

"I'm not taking anybody's—"

"John says he agrees with you," he told her. "He says it's one of his all-time favorite movies. Every time he sees it he breaks down weeping—*sobbing*, he says."

"Good for you, John!" she called out.

"Well, you just made your aunt Ro a very happy woman. You oughta see her face. She's got this glow coming out. Can you picture it?"

"A glow, right."

"Tell you something, she's one hell of a gal."

"She definitely is," I said.

"You think I don't know that? After seven years?"

"No, I think you do."

"You're goddam right I do. But let me ask you something. You didn't really cry, did you?"

"What, at the movie? At *Wuthering Heights* you mean?"

"Did you really break down weeping?"

I thought of that scene near the end, which always got to me, Heathcliff standing over Catherine's deathbed, telling her corpse to haunt him for the rest of his life, crying out from the depths of his soul, *Torment me! Drive me mad! Only, do not leave me in this dark alone, where I cannot find you!* I gave a laugh. "Yeah, right, Uncle Doug. *Buckets*," I said.

"He's laughing," he told Aunt Ro. "That tickled him." Then, to me: "You're all right, John. You know that, don't you?"

"Thanks, Uncle Doug," I said, a little glow of my own going now.

"Okay, well, listen, I gotta go," he told me. "Got some work to do. Know what I'm doing? Take a guess."

"Building shelves?"

"Putting in a garden."

"Really? A garden? That's really . . . something."

"Out in the back. Just a little patch. Know what I'm growing there? Take a guess. Go ahead."

"Well . . ."

"You'll never guess. But go ahead."

"Daffodils?"

There was this silence. Then he said quietly, "What're ya, trying to be a smartass now?"

"*No.* I just . . . you said I'd never guess so I was trying to think of something I would never . . . you know . . . guess."

"Carrots," he said.

"You're kidding. Really? That's a great vegetable. In fact that's probably one of my favorite—"

"All right, John. I'm hanging up now."

"I *love* carrots, Uncle Doug."

He hung up.

LADIES AND GENTLEMEN,
MR. LEONARD COHEN

Out walking around one evening in early spring trying to clear my head, I came to a little movie house off Clark Street and stood there staring at the marquee:

8:00: Ladies and Gentlemen, Mr. Leonard Cohen, a documentary

It was only about seven, so I went walking around some more, at a snappier pace now. I was excited. A movie about Leonard Cohen!

I thought about the first time I'd ever heard him, or even heard of him. It was in a modern poetry class, taught by Dr. Ledbetter, who was young and wore turtleneck sweaters. One morning he played a tape for us, something by a Canadian poet-singer-songwriter Leonard Cohen, a song called "Suzanne." First you heard a pensive guitar for a few notes, and then this nasal droning voice began singing quietly:

Suzanne takes you down to her place near the river . . .

The voice went on, in its intimate way, about tea and oranges from China, Jesus in his lonely wooden tower, the sun pouring down like honey, while Suzanne in rags and feathers held the mirror . . .

I didn't know exactly what he was getting at but the song almost put me into a trance, it was so beautiful and mysterious and sad. Afterwards, Dr. Ledbetter broke it all down for us, everyone scribbling in their notebooks, but I was wishing he would just leave it alone.

The record store owner I spoke to later over the phone had never heard of any Leonard Cohen. "What is he?"

"How do you mean?"

"Folk? Rock? Blues? R and B?"

"Hard to say. He's Canadian, I know *that*."

He took my number and a week or so later he phoned and said he had something called *The Songs of Leonard Cohen*.

What a perfect title.

And what a perfect face he had. It was on the cover, a perfect poet's face, long and sad and deeply sincere. I ran with it all the way back to my dorm, and was so glad Larry wasn't in.

Suzanne takes you down to her place near the river . . .

I walked up and down between the two beds, loving every song, every sad lovely one of them, both sides. Some of the lyrics gave me trouble, a lot of them in fact, but I understood his voice, the place it came from, deep inside, deep down, where it hurt:

If your life is a leaf that the seasons tear off and condemn . . .

I was playing the whole thing over again when Larry came barging in. I said to him, "Hi! Hey, what's up?" I felt embarrassed, like I'd been caught.

"What the hell is that?" he said, meaning the music.

"Oh, just . . . something somebody gave me. I was just checking it out."

"Sounds like he's fucking dying, man."

I laughed. "Doesn't he?"

"Somebody gave you that?"

"Some chick." I took it off.

After that, I only played it when I knew for certain Larry wouldn't be back for a long while, Saturday nights for example.

Since then, Leonard Cohen had put out two more albums just as good, cutting just as deep, and he still meant just as much to me, with his off-key voice and his long sad poet's face.

When I got back to the theater it was still a little early and I hung around outside, smoking. Maybe there'd be a small, sad-eyed girl in a raincoat and we would recognize each other immediately and go in and sit together.

She didn't show. Hardly anyone did. I went in just before it started and took an aisle seat in the back. The lights were lowered. I sat up straighter.

The movie turned out to be pretty old, all about the *early* Leonard Cohen, before the songs, when he was still just a poet. It showed a crowded city street, where I picked him out right away, in a trench coat, hands deep in the pockets, and as the camera moved in closer the narrator said, "Leonard Cohen is a poet."

It showed him crossing the street.

"He is a constant wanderer."

It showed him gazing at a female mannequin.

"He has an enormous curiosity . . ."

It showed him gazing at a movie poster.

". . . and a hypersensitivity."

It showed him gazing at the gray sky.

I didn't understand—were we supposed to think he didn't notice the camera a few feet away from his long sad face?

"Cohen works his talent very hard."

He was at a desk now, laboring over a poem.

"He writes for several hours a day."

He looked off, tapping his mouth with his pen.

"He writes . . ."

He wrote something.

". . . and rewrites."

He crumpled up the paper and began again.

I couldn't take any more of this.

Outside I went walking around, walking fast, head down. But the camera had followed me out, the narrator intoning, "He is a constant wanderer . . ."

I headed back to my apartment. When I got in, I set a pan of water on the stove and dropped a hot dog into it. While I was waiting I put some music on, his second album, *Songs from a Room*, just to see.

Like a bird on the wire,

Like a drunk in a midnight choir . . .

Well, I still liked the guy. How could you not? He probably knew he was partly full of shit, probably knew better than anyone.

I have tried, in my way, to be free.

THE EXORCIST

I was asleep when the phone by the bed went off. I sat up and looked at the clock: 2:45 a.m.

"Hello?" I said carefully.

A raspy voice shouted, *"Yourmothersuckscocksinhell!"*

"What? I'm sorry, my what? I didn't—"

"Your mother!"

"What about her?"

"Sucks cocks!"

"My mother . . ."

"In Hell!"

I didn't understand. "Do you *know* my mother?"

No response.

"Who is this?"

"Satan."

"Right," I said, "okay," and told him to go to hell. But as I was putting the phone down I could hear him shouting in there, *"Wait, don't hang up, don't hang up!"*

I couldn't, somehow. "Who *is* this."

"It's not really Satan," he admitted in a normal voice—he sounded about seventeen. "You don't know me. I dialed whatever. You're whatever. I didn't mean that about your mother, it just came out. It's from the movie. Have you seen it yet? I've seen it five times."

"What movie. What're you talking about?"

"*The Exorcist*. You haven't *seen* it?"

"No." I'd seen previews and it looked pretty scary but not in a very enjoyable way.

"Listen to this," he said. "I can speak backwards. Check it out: 'Natas si eman ym.' Know what I just said? 'My . . . name . . . is . . . Satan.'"

Okay, I instructed myself, *just be nice, and get off.* "That's pretty good," I told him.

"Thanks."

"But I'm afraid I have to go now," I added.

"Can I tell you a secret?"

"It's very late."

"I have to tell *some*one."

"Maybe another time."

"Please?"

"Be quick," I told him.

"I've got all the symptoms: bedwetting, speaking backwards, green vomit, levitation, evil thoughts—you wouldn't believe some of the shit I think about doing."

"Like prank phone calls?"

"This isn't a prank, it's a cry for help, asshole."

"Okay, that's it. Goodnight."

"Right. Go back to bed. In the morning you'll think you had this dream about some fucked-up guy thinks he's possessed by the devil, calls you up wanting to know if you'd like to go see a movie some time. Would you, by the way? Just curious."

I wasn't sure I understood. "Are you asking me out?"

"Yes or no, pal. What's it gonna be?"

"It's gonna be no," I told him.

"Well, *that's* a relief," he said. "Know what I do to fags? What I'd like to do? Wanna hear?"

"I'm hanging up now, okay? Goodnight."

"*Wait.* Know what happens? Satan leaves the little girl and gets inside the priest, the young one, so you know what he does? Jumps out the window and breaks his neck. He didn't have any choice! See what I'm saying? What I'm tryna say?"

Ah shit, I thought. "So that's what *you're* gonna do?"

"What, jump out the window? Right, I'd fall about three feet, ya dumb fuck. I'm sorry, that was way outa line. You mad at me now?"

"Listen . . ."

"Oh don't say 'listen' like that. I hate when people tell me to listen. Why don't *they* ever listen? Go ahead. You were saying."

I told him carefully, "Quit, seeing, the stupid, fucking, movie."

"It's not stupid, *you're* stupid. People don't think there's a devil but that's what he *wants* them to think. Know what she does? The little girl? Masturbates with a crucifix. Does that turn you on? If it does, you are one sick fuck, my friend. Plus she barfs green vomit in his face, and her head turns allll the way around, and when he flings holy water on her it *burns*, it *burns*. You gotta go see it."

"Yeah well, meanwhile I think maybe you should go see something a little more lighthearted, y'know? A little upbeat?"

"Like what."

"*I* don't know . . ." I tried to think. "*Singin' in the Rain* or something."

He laughed. "*Singin' in the Rain?*"

"Something *like* that, I'm saying."

"How *old* are you, man?"

"All right, y'know what? It's going on three o'clock in the goddam—"

"Wanna go together? See something together? A musical comedy? Whaddaya say?"

"No. I'm sorry."

"Want me to jump out the window?"

"It's only three feet," I reminded him.

"Want me to hang myself?"

"Look . . ."

"Oh don't say 'look' like that. I hate when people tell me to look. What's your name, by the way. Can you tell me *that* much?"

I didn't see any harm. "John," I said.

"Mine's Luke, short for Lucifer. Not really. So what's your number, John? I don't even remember what I dialed."

Thank you, Jesus, I thought.

"Lemme grab a pen," he told me. "Okay, go ahead."

"Y'know?" I said, as if having thought it over. "I think I'd probably rather not."

He didn't say anything for a moment. Then: "Why do you hate me?"

"I don't hate you. I don't even—"

"Can't you understand? It's not me, it's him. It's *him*."

Satan, he apparently meant. I told him as nicely as I could, "I really think you need to go talk to someone, Luke."

"I *am* talking to someone, I'm talking to you. Aren't you someone?"

"I was thinking more like, you know, someone professional."

"Like a shrink, you mean?"

"Well . . ."

"I don't need a shrink, I need a fucking *priest*, you dickwad."

"Well I'm *not* a fucking priest, all right? So—"

"Fine. You're off the hook. Go on, go back to bed. Goodnight. Goodbye."

"Wait," I told him.

He waited. "Well?" he said.

"So how 's it end?" I asked.

"What, the movie?"

"What happens?"

"I told you, the priest jumps out the window, breaks his neck."

"What about the little girl?"

"She's fine. All smiles. Doesn't even remember."

"*Well* then," I said to him, putting a smile in my voice. "See? Happy ending. It was looking pretty grim there for a *while*, right? Pretty dark?"

"Yeah?"

"But then, finally, somehow, everything all worked out, didn't it."

"So what's your point."

"I'm *saying*, it just goes to show: things have a way of . . . you know . . ."

"Working out?"

"'All smiles,' you said. The little girl was 'all smiles.'"

He was quiet for a moment, like he was thinking. Then he said, "What're you, some kinda nutcase?"

"Excuse me?"

He spoke carefully: "It's a *movie*, man. Okay? We're talking about a fucking *movie*."

"Yeah and a pretty idiotic one, *I'd* say."

"Fuck you, you haven't even seen it."

"Well, it *sounds* idiotic—green vomit and the rest."

"*Pancake* batter, okay? Okay?"

"That's what they used? Pancake batter?"

"With green food coloring, okay?"

"Huh." I admitted that was kind of interesting.

"She gets him right in the face, man." He started laughing now. "The shit's all over his fuckin' glasses, and the mother's like, 'Oh, hey, sorry about that, Father.'" Laughing harder he managed to ask me, "Whaddaya say? Wanna go? It's kind of a comedy actually, lotta slapstick, kind of a musical comedy."

"There's singing?"

"Not as *such*. Anyway, how 'bout it, wanna go?"

"Not really."

He was quiet.

"Sorry," I added.

"Yeah, you're sorry all right, you're about the sorriest—by the way, did I mention? Your mother sucks cocks in Hell."

"So you said."

"Your own mother! Sucks cocks!"

"Okay, Luke."

"In *Hell!*"

We were quiet, both of us.

Then I said to him, "Y'know, speaking of memorable lines? I'm reminded of a pretty good one, a pretty *profound* one actually. It's from the final scene in one of my all-time favorite—"

"Hey man, it's three in the fuckin morning," he informed me, and hung up.

HIGH NOON

There was this barber I was going to, a big relaxed guy named Fred, owner of Friendly Fred's, a little one-chair shop a couple blocks from my apartment, and he was friendly to all his *other* customers, telling jokes, gabbing about the weather, sports, politics, his car troubles, his *wife* troubles, or whatever was on the little TV by the window—the Cubs game, *General Hospital*—but when *I* got in the chair he'd say, "How ya want it?" and that would be it, not another word the entire haircut.

Or else—and this is what really pissed me off—if a customer was waiting, reading a magazine, while I was in the chair? Fred would talk to *him*, sometimes even stepping away from my head for emphasis:

"I don't suppose you heard about those astronauts that found a restaurant on the moon, did you?"

"No, Fred," the guy would say. "Tell me about it."

"Well, it seems the *food* was all right . . ."

"Yeah?"

"But the place didn't have much atmosphere."

Big laugh from the guy, Fred returning to my head, chuckling, repeating the punch line: "Said the place just didn't seem to have much atmosphere."

And if *I* responded—"That's pretty funny," or, "That's a good one, Fred"—here's what he would say:

"Beg pardon?"

This finally started getting to me.

"I mean, what's his problem?" I said to my older sister Cheryl, over the phone.

"I wouldn't read too much into it."

"What he *got* against me?"

"It's probably not even *about* you, John."

"I just don't get it."

"What about tipping him?"

"Pay him to talk to me?"

"You don't tip him, right?"

"Of course not."

"Maybe that's all it is."

"A tip."

"Try it next time."

"What, fifty cents?"

"Give him a couple dollars."

"Jesus, Cheryl."

"Just to see. But meanwhile?"

"'Try not to obsess,' right."

So after the next haircut, after giving him his seven dollars, I said, "And here's a little extra for ya, Fred," handing over two more ones. "Now, don't spend it all in one place," I added, with a laugh.

"Beg pardon?"

"I was just saying, don't . . . you know . . ."

He waited, his head cocked to one side.

"Never mind," I told him, and walked out.

"Felt like a goddam fool, Cheryl."

"What about just going to another barber—is that an option?"

"Okay but see, that would be admitting this whole thing bothers me. And it doesn't, not really. So my barber won't talk to me. Big deal. What'm I, desperate?"

"All the same, wouldn't it be a lot—"

"It just bothers me, that's all. I mean, what have I done to him? What horrible thing?"

"You're giving this guy too much power, John."

"Or is it just my essence he despises."

"Way too much power."

Another thing. I'd been seeing Fred every few weeks for about six months now, and every time I sat in the chair he would ask me, "How ya want it?" And my answer was always the same: "Just a trim."

"How ya want it?"

"Just a trim."

Every time.

So wouldn't you think by now, instead of asking me how I want it, he would say something like, "The usual?" I mean, even if he wasn't going to talk to me, wouldn't you think he'd at least acknowledge that he's actually seen me before? But every time I sat in the chair it was like I *fell* there from the moon—where those astronauts found that restaurant.

I told Cheryl I was beginning to feel like maybe I really was from the fucking moon.

"Listen," she said, "I was thinking . . ."

"Like some kind of alien, you know?"

"What if you tried talking to *him*?"

"A stranger in a strange land."

"John?"

"What."

"I was saying, what if *you* tried talking to *him*."

"How do you mean?"

"Just, you know, ask him how he's he doing. 'How ya doin', Fred?'"

"Right. He'll say, 'Beg pardon?'"

"So then you try again. You say, 'I was just wondering, how's it going?'"

"Force the issue, you're saying."

"Not belligerently, but—"

"Firmly, right. I like that. Let's try it. 'How ya doin,' Fred?'"

"'Beg pardon?'"

"'I *said*—'"

"No, John, see . . ."

"Right, right."

So the next time I went I took Cheryl's advice and tried talking to him. It took me a while. There was no one else in the shop so it was utterly silent, not even the television, just the sound of his scissors. I sat there struggling through almost the entire haircut. Then finally, as he was combing me down, I said to him, "So. How ya doin', Fred?"

"Beg pardon?"

"I was just, you know, wondering . . ."

"Yeah?"

"How's it going?"

"How's what going?"

"Well . . . your *car*, for one thing."

"How's my car going?"

"Running okay?"

"Running fine. Why?"

"Well . . . I was thinking about buying it."

"It's not for sale."

"I don't blame ya, car that runs that good? Hey, how 'bout those Cubbies."

"What about 'em?"

Cubs were baseball and it was the middle of winter, it was *snowing* out. "Never mind," I told him.

He finished up. And when he swung the chair around to face the big mirror, holding the little mirror behind my head, I said what I always said to him: "Fine, Fred. Thanks."

He removed the sheet. I got down, gave him his money, grabbed my coat off the wall and was walking towards the door. But then I stopped and turned around. "By the way, I won't be back," I told him.

He nodded, putting the money in the register.

I stood there. My heart was pounding. "But I would like to know just one little thing, Fred."

"Oh?"

"What exactly is your problem?"

He looked at me.

"Will you tell me please?" I said. "What have you got against me?"

He shut the register drawer. "You want to know?"

I nodded. "I want to know."

He stepped over to the chair, sat in it, folded his hands in his lap and looked at me. "First time you ever came in here. Do you remember?"

I tried to think. "Not really. Remember what."

He looked at me a long moment. Then he said, "You told me, 'Shhh.'"

I stood there. "I told you . . . to be quiet?"

"'Shhh.' That's what you said to me."

"I don't understand. Why would I want you to be quiet?"

He nodded towards the little TV. "You were watching a movie."

"Ah."

"You were in the chair. I was telling you a joke. Got about halfway through. You put up your finger. 'Shhh,' you said."

I remembered now. "It was *High Noon*," I said, "right?"

"I don't know what *time* it was, that's not the point."

"No, I mean the movie, that was the movie, *High Noon*."

He shook his head. "Doesn't matter. This isn't a movie theater, it's a barber shop. A *friendly* barber shop. Like the old-*time* barber shops. Where you'd visit with people. Swap jokes, tell stories, give your opinion. One guy says this, other one says that, but *no*body—understand?—*no*body says to *any*body, 'Shhh.'"

I stepped closer. I said to him, "Fred? I do understand. And I want to apologize. I want to say right here, right now, I am very, very sorry."

"Fine," he said, nodding. "Okay, then. That's all I'm asking for."

"You had every reason to be angry."

"That's all right."

"No, Fred, it's not. It's really not. I mean, let's face it," I said, pointing towards the television, "when we start choosing make-be*lieve* life over—"

The little bells on a strap above the door sounded, as someone walked in.

"*There* he is," Fred said to him, hopping out of the chair.

"Hey, Fred. How you been?" said the guy, hanging up his coat.

"Oh, can't complain," Fred admitted. "Hey listen, tell me something."

"What's that," said the guy, heading to the chair.

"You the son of a bitch ordered all this snow?"

The guy gave a laugh and said, "Not me, old buddy," settling into the chair like into a warm bath.

Cheryl couldn't get over it: "That . . . is so . . ."

"Isn't it? Isn't it?"

"All this time . . ."

"He was hurt. I hurt the guy."

"You didn't mean to."

"But still. 'Shhh.' Y'know? So insulting."

"You probably weren't even aware."

"Probably not. Watching a movie—a *movie*, Cheryl. I mean, let's face it, when we start choosing make-believe life over—"

"What was it, by the way."

"The movie?"

"Do you remember?"

"*High Noon*. Ever see it?"

"Is that Gregory Peck?"

"Gary Cooper."

"He's a sheriff?"

"Marshall. You've seen it, I'm sure."

"I don't think so. Just clips."

"*The* great cowboy movie of all time. The lone hero, standing tall, doing what he's gotta do."

"Is there a big showdown scene?"

"Out on the empty street, sun beating down."

"High noon."

"Truth time, Cheryl. Little bit like today, you know? In a way? Sort of?"

"Well, I'm glad you finally confronted him."

"I was heading out the door. Running away, right? There's a scene early on, where he's racing out of town in a wagon with his bride, just married . . ."

"Maureen O'Hara?"

"Grace Kelly. So he gets out of town, but then all of a sudden he pulls up the horses, whoa, and says something like, 'They're makin' me run away. I've never run away from *anybody*.' And so, of course . . ."

"He heads back."

"I was at the door, Cheryl. I was leaving. For good. Putting my hand on the knob. But then I stopped, turned around . . ."

"And faced him."

"Yep."

We were quiet for a moment.

"Will you go back, you think? Next haircut?"

"I don't know. Might be kind of awkward."

She agreed.

GONE WITH THE WIND

My mother claims to have been the very first person in line at its very first showing in Chicago, at the Chicago Theater, nine o'clock on a spring morning, her best friend, Eleanor, second in line.

Mildred and Eleanor, 1939.

They were telephone operators, working the night shift at Bell on Washington Boulevard, and that morning, instead of going home, decided to go see Clark Gable and Vivien Leigh in the Old South.

They had to wait an hour for the ticket booth to open, but it was a fine spring morning—I picture laundered-looking sunlight on the tall buildings—and they chatted and shared an egg salad sandwich.

My mother doesn't remember where they got the sandwich, but she said it was delicious, eating it outside like that, right on the street.

Meanwhile the line behind them kept growing, until it went all the way down the block and around the corner.

Then finally a girl appeared in the ticket booth—looking bored, chewing a wad of gum—and my mother stepped up, money in hand: "One, please."

Holding her ticket, she waited for Eleanor.

Then Mildred and Eleanor walked together through the immaculate, red-carpeted lobby without stopping for popcorn. An usher wearing white gloves was opening a pair of large doors—just for them, it seemed.

They entered the dim theater and headed bouncily down the tilted aisle, all the way down, and sat themselves in the middle of the very first row, shiny black purses in their laps, heads back, waiting for the curtain to open:

There was a curtain.

And when, at last, it began to slide open I picture my mother clutching Eleanor's arm.

Thirty-five years later on a rainy Sunday afternoon I saw it at a little theater off Clark Street, with a bad hangover and nothing better to do. Sitting in the very last row, feet up, I counted eighteen other people scattered around, like at a porn flick.

There wasn't a curtain.

I fell asleep during a gala affair at Scarlett's cousin's house. Two and a half hours later an usher shook me by the arm, telling me the movie was over, telling me I had to leave.

Out on the sidewalk the rain had stopped and the sun was shining horribly bright.

TAXI DRIVER

I was back living in the old neighborhood, Riverdale, drinking a lot, most evenings in a loud little bar called Nick's. Sometimes, when I got drunk, I loved everyone and would even put my arm around a guy's shoulder and tell him what a terrific fellow he was. Other nights, I would start looking for a fight, or at least a good loud argument. It could be over anything, Cubs versus Sox, the Virgin Birth, where to find really good pizza. One night I got into it with this big round shaggy guy, Donny Malloy, over who was the better actor, Pacino or DeNiro.

I'd seen *Taxi Driver* three times and told Donny to please try and be serious, Pacino wasn't even in the same fucking league as DeNiro, didn't he know that?

Donny shook his head in amazement, telling me I was so full of shit he didn't know where to begin, maybe with *Dog Day Afternoon*.

We went back and forth like that for a while, Siskel and Ebert, and then he said he had to go take a leak. I told him go ahead, take your leak.

By that time, we'd had a couple shots with our beers and I was never very good at that, so, while Donny was in the john, I went out by the parking lot and threw up in a bush and felt better. Then I found my car and sat on the hood and lit a cigarette. It was a nice night, quite a lot of stars up there. I smoked and thought about the universe, how big it was, how small we were, just a speck. I whispered something from *Taxi Driver*: "'I'm God's lonely man.'"

I decided to call it a night.

A couple days later I ran into Donny again, at Nick's. He was sitting at a stool with this lanky guy called Birdman, watching the Cubs game. I came over, wanting to explain about taking off the other night in the middle of our discussion. I put my hands on their backs and said, "Gentlemen."

They turned and looked at me. Birdman gave me a little nod and turned back to the game. Donny didn't even give me that. I figured he was mad about the other night—he was very temperamental that way—but when I asked if they were ready for another beer he said, "I don't drink with thiefs."

I wasn't sure I'd heard him. "What did you say?"

He said it again, "I don't drink with thiefs."

I turned to Birdman. "What's he talking about?"

He shrugged, eyes on the Cub game.

I grabbed Donny's arm. "What're you talking about?"

He turned to me. "I'll tell you what I'm talking about, I'm talking about the other night."

"What about it."

"I went to the john?"

"Yeah?"

"I come back?"

"Yeah?"

"The twenty I left under my glass?"

"What about it."

"It's gone. And so are you."

It took me a moment to say anything. "And you think . . . I took it?"

He shook his big round head: "I don't *think* you took it, I *know* you did."

I looked at Birdman. He was still watching the Cub game, or pretending to. I looked back at Donny. "Are you calling me a thief?"

He pointed at me. "You catch on fast." He turned back to the game.

Standing there, trying not to sink under this, I put out this laugh, this very lame laugh, and gave Birdman a backhanded whack on the arm. "You believe this fuckin' guy?"

I didn't mean it as an actual question but he answered it. "Yeah," he said, eyes on the game, "I think I do."

Probably because of the clammy way I was acting, like a thief who's been caught.

Meanwhile, the other guys in the bar all heard this, heard Donny calling me a thief to my face, so now they were waiting to see what I was going to do about it. I had to do something, otherwise it would look like I agreed, like I was a thief. But all I did was keep standing there, like a thief who's been caught. And the more I knew I looked like one, the more I really felt like one, and the harder it was to do anything but stand there.

I finally just turned around and walked out.

When I got to my apartment, I sat on the edge of the couch. I didn't even take my jacket off, I just sat there: a thief. That's what Donny declared I was, and now after walking out like I did, that's what they all believed, and would tell anyone who missed it:

Hey, you know Manderino?

What about him?

Guy's a fucking thief.

Nawww. Really?

He ripped off Donny Malloy, right here in the bar.

You're shittin' me.

I ain't shittin' ya.

And that would never change, no matter what I did. For instance I could save a fourteen year-old girl from a life of prostitution, like DeNiro did in *Taxi Driver*, get shot up for my trouble, it's in all the papers, big hero. They'd say, *Yeah, but you know? He's still a fucking thief.*

I got up from the couch. I went out to my car and drove back to Nick's. On the way, I put together a little speech. I went over it a couple of times.

Donny was still there, watching the Cubs game along with everyone else. They all looked very settled in, like it was a fact, over and done with: *Manderino's a thief. And now, back to the Cubbies.*

So my job was to *unsettle* them.

I walked straight up behind Donny and laid a heavy hand on his shoulder. He turned around, looking surprised to see me.

"Here," I told him, holding up a twenty-dollar bill, and gave my little speech, loud for everyone to hear: "I never stole anything in my life, but if you think I took your twenty dollars here's twenty dollars and if you ever call me a thief again I'll kick your ass, understood?"

He gave this amused little grin. Then he took the bill and held it up to the light. "Yep," he said, "this looks like the one," and got a laugh from the audience.

"It's not," I assured him.

"Tell you what," he said, and leaned forward, holding the bill in front of my face. "I'll take this back on one condition: you admit you stole it. I'll even buy you a beer with it, how's that."

I shook my head, no. "I didn't take your fucking money, Malloy. I don't know who did, but it wasn't me."

He sat back, elbows on the bar, nodding, hamming it up. "I see. So now you're blaming one of *these* guys, is that it?" Then he suddenly sat forward again. "Well, let me tell you something. These guys are my friends. You saying my friends are thiefs?"

That put me on the spot. So I said to him, "Look. First of all, the word is 'thieves,' okay? Not 'thiefs.'"

"Well," he said, crumbling the twenty into a ball, "you

117

oughta know," and tossed it off my forehead. "Now get outa here, ya fuckin' thief."

I'd already warned him if he ever called me a thief again I would kick his ass, so everyone was waiting.

First, though, I couldn't help doing this little DeNiro thing. "You talkin' to *me*?" I said, and looked over my shoulder like maybe he was talking to someone behind me, then looked at him again, tilting my head in a questioning way, pointing at myself: "You talkin' to *me*?"

He held up his palms and lifted his shoulders—maybe that was something from Pacino—and said, "You're the only thief in here."

I folded my arms and looked off, nodding my head—more DeNiro—saying quietly, "Okay . . . okay . . ." Then I suddenly unfolded my arms, reared back and punched him in the jaw just as hard as I possibly could. He fell backwards, cracking his head against the bar, dropped to the floor and lay there on his side, eyes closed, not moving at all.

Everyone was quiet. The only sound was the Cubs announcer: "Having himself quite a night, with the bat *and* the glove . . ."

I stood there waiting for Donny to move, even just his hand, even just a finger.

"There's a deep drive down the right field line, curving . . . curving . . ."

I got the hell out of there.

Driving home I didn't think, just drove the car. I didn't think until I was sitting once again on the edge of the couch, staring straight ahead, running the zipper of my jacket up and down, up and down: *Oh God, oh fuck, oh Jesus, I killed him, I didn't mean to, I was in a movie, I was acting in a movie, but it wasn't a movie and now he's dead, he's actually dead, I killed him, I'm a murderer, I murdered Donny Malloy, took away his life, the whole rest of his life, stole it from him, I'm a murderer and a thief . . .*

I wanted so bad for the credits to be rolling now, for this to be a stupid, overly dramatic movie. But it wasn't. The cops would be here soon, *real* ones.

I quickly straightened up the apartment a little, then sat on the couch again, hands on my knees, and waited.

Ten minutes later, I heard footsteps coming up the long hallway.

I waited.

They kept coming, then stopped on the other side of the door. There was a knock, just one loud knock.

"Yes," I said, "I'm here," and got up, and walked over, and opened the door.

Donny punched me in the jaw.

I staggered back and he followed me in and punched me in the stomach, then punched me in the jaw again. I went down so he wouldn't punch me anymore. He stood over me for a moment, catching his breath. Then he kicked me in the ribs—not very hard, more of a gesture—and walked out, slamming the door behind him.

I stayed there on the floor. There was blood in my mouth, warm and sweet. I felt so happy I wanted to weep. And in fact I did, laying my head in my arms, calling myself God's lonely man.

CLOSE ENCOUNTERS OF THE THIRD KIND

Molly was small and pretty and shy and I loved her name—
it was on her Dairy Queen blouse. I stopped there every
evening after work that summer, and if the other girl came
to the window I told her, "That's okay, I'll wait for Molly."
And when she came she always said hi and smiled. I would
order a vanilla cone, one scoop, and make small talk while
she fixed it. I had secret plans for us. I had that song in my
head all the time:

> *Just Molly and me*
> *And baby makes three,*
> *We're happy in my blue heaven.*

First, though, I had to ask her out. So I finally did, and
she said, "Um . . . okay."

She still lived with her parents. When I picked her up, I
had to come in.

"This is my mom and this is my dad."

They were on the couch, *Barney Miller* on.

"Hello," I said to them, nodding, smiling.

"Nice to meet you," the mother said.

"Going to a movie, huh?" the father said.

"Yes," I said, "a movie, right."

"Well, you have yourselves a nice time," the mother said.

"Thank you," I said. "We will."

"Don't be too late," the father told Molly, and glanced at me.

"I won't," Molly promised.

"It was very nice meeting you," the mother said.

"Nice meeting *you*," I told them both.

Walking to the car I said to Molly, "They seem awfully nice."

"Uh-huh."

As I drove us to the Dolton Theater, she told me about her cat Samantha giving birth to three kittens that morning.

I told her the Egyptians used to worship cats.

She said she didn't know that.

I said it was true.

We passed the Dairy Queen. "There it is," I said.

She told me an idea she had for a new ice cream flavor, featuring peanut butter and honey.

I told her that sounded awful, and we both laughed.

This was going great.

At the theater, she didn't want any popcorn so I didn't either and we sat together waiting for the movie to begin.

I told her this was about UFO's.

She knew that.

I asked her if she believed in UFO's.

She said she wasn't sure.

I told her that was a very good answer.

We sat there.

I asked her if she'd ever heard that song, "My Blue Heaven."

She didn't think so.

The movie started. I laid my arm along the back of her seat.

About ten minutes later, I was about to very casually move my arm onto her shoulder, but just then she opened the purse in her lap and I watched from the corner of my eye as she lifted out a dark little bottle, unscrewed the cap and took a sip. I could smell it: *Robitussin.* I figured she must be working on a cough. My arm was going to sleep and I brought it back.

About ten minutes later, she opened her purse again and took another hit.

I whispered, "Is that . . . are you . . ."

"For my cough," she whispered, putting the bottle back.

Halfway through the movie, she'd had six little hits and was now responding out loud to events on the screen, saying things like, "Whoa," and "Aw, maaan?" And by the end of the movie, when those anemic-looking little doe-eyed aliens came walking delicately down the ramp of their space ship, Molly said loudly, "Oh, *look* at them, *look* at them . . ."

Afterwards, walking to the car, she was weaving and talking away. "What a movie. God, you know? I wish that would happen to me. I wish somebody from outer space, some cute little people like that . . . I would go with them, I wouldn't even hesitate, I'd say 'Let's *blow* this popstand.'"

As soon as we got in the car she opened her purse and took out the bottle of cough medicine.

"How can you drink that stuff, Molly?"

"For my cough." She took a hit. "Here," she said, and held out the bottle.

"No, thanks. Listen, don't take any more tonight, okay? Your parents are gonna be pretty—"

"Start the car. C'mon. Let's go."

"All right but . . . what did you feel like doing? Get something to eat? A pizza or something?"

"Nah. Just drive around. Go 'head. Start the car."

I started the car.

"Attaboy."

I pulled out of the lot.

"Hey, y'know?" she said. "I wish . . . man, I wish something like that would happen to me."

"A close encounter?"

"That would be so fucking great."

We drove around. She talked some more about how much she would like to be abducted by aliens. I tried to change the subject. I asked her what she planned to do with her cat Samantha's kittens.

"They're so *little*," she said. "You should see, they're so . . . *little*," and she started crying.

I didn't know what to do. I put out my arm for her to move under it and she did, laying her head against me. I told her, "They'll be fine, Molly."

"They're so tiny."

"They'll be fine. Really. Don't worry. They're gonna be just—"

"Hey," she said, no longer crying. "Want a *really* close encounter? Of the *fourth* kind?" She started fumbling with my belt buckle.

"What're you doing?"

She kept working away. "What's it look like?"

"Will ya stop? Jesus."

She sat up and looked at me. "S'matter? You queer?"

"I just don't think you're in your right . . . you know . . ."

"Miiind, you mean? My right miiind?"

I missed the little Dairy Queen girl.

"That shit you've been drinking..."

"I told you, it's for my cough."

"You don't have a cough, you haven't coughed all—"

"See? It works. C'mon," she said, and put her hand on my leg. "Don't be such a homo."

"Maybe some other time," I told her.

"What'sa matter, don'tcha like me?"

"I like you a lot, Molly."

"Do you think I'm nice?"

"I think you're very nice, yes."

"Do you love me?"

"Well . . . I mean . . ."

"Want me to *make* you love me? I can *make* you love me," she said, and went after my belt buckle again, just as I was making a turn, and she fell onto my lap.

"Molly, get off! I can't steer!"

She also had her feet in the way of the brake pedal and we went over a curb, then onto a lawn while I kept kicking and stomping and was finally able to stop the car, sending both of us against the steering wheel.

"Whoa, fuck," she said, and sat up.

We were three feet away from a large picture window, on the other side of which, across a stretch of carpet, a family of four—Mom, Dad, Bud and Sis—were arranged on a couch, staring bug-eyed into my headlights.

We sat there staring back at them.

"They prob'ly think we're aliens," Molly whispered.

I snapped out of it, backed off of their lawn, got out on the street again and resumed driving around.

She was quiet now. So was I. I kept picturing them—Mom and Dad and Bud and Sis—returning without comment to their television show, a sitcom, staring at it for ten seconds, then all of them laughing together briefly, stopping together, staring for another ten seconds, then laughing together . . .

I didn't want that, I decided. No, thank you. I didn't want any part of that. I told Molly I could see her point about wanting to be abducted by aliens. I told her *I* wouldn't mind it either, not a bit. "I'm with *you*," I said. "Life down here is getting just a little bit too—"

"Drive me home please?" she said quietly.

"Yours, you mean?"

"Yes, please."

She was sitting forward, head lowered, her hand braced against the glove box.

"What's the matter?" I asked.

"I don't feel so good."

"Well?" I said. "See?"

"Fuck you," she said.

I drove her home. We didn't speak. But I was thinking. And as I pulled up in front of her house I said, "Y'know, Molly, there's a lot of ways we can look at tonight, a lot of different—"

"Thank you, I had a nice time," she said, and got out.

I watched her walking carefully towards the front porch. Her father opened the door and I pulled away.

JASON AND THE ARGONAUTS

I'm in a Motel 6, somewhere in the middle of Nebraska, on my way to the West Coast where I intend to finally break free and live. It's one o'clock in the morning. I was almost asleep, but then a woman on the other side of the wall started moaning and groaning while a man began grunting and muttering, the two of them laboring on and on. So now I'm sitting on the edge of the bed in my underwear watching TV. The room still smells like the turkey sub I ate three hours ago.

Jason, brave and clean and handsome, is battling the seven-headed Hydra, his dark-eyed girlfriend, Medea, looking on, concerned. Jason manages to stab the creature in the heart, causing all the heads to go wheeling around on their long necks rather comically, and I laugh, hear myself laughing alone in a motel room in the middle of the night in the middle of Nebraska, and stop laughing.

The Hydra finally falls on all its faces. Jason grabs the Golden Fleece and with Medea goes running towards the sea where the *Argo* is anchored. But wait—skeleton warriors come sprouting out of the ground, equipped with swords and shields, Jason clearly wondering: *How the hell do you kill skeletons?*

Answer: lop off their heads.

Back on the *Argo*, he kisses Medea passionately. Then they look at one another—*gaze* at one another—and kiss again, music up.

The End.

I turn it off and go walking around the room, smoking, telling myself this is the right thing for me to be doing, this was a good decision, wise and brave. Colorful adventures lie ahead. Just keep heading westward. Jason himself said it best: *There's no turning back on this voyage.*

I jab out my cigarette, get back into bed, close my eyes— and there they go again, her with the groaning, him with the grunting, the bedsprings wheezing away. I want to pound on the wall. I want to get up on my knees, pound on the wall and holler, *For God sakes, put something into it!*

GOING NATIVE

Interior: Nearly empty fern bar in L.A., late afternoon, Jack drinking a beer, writing in his notebook, only other patron a woman around forty in a yellow dress—sun dress?—three stools down, sipping a pina colada from a straw. Bartender tall and skinny, little green stud in his earlobe—gay?—leaning near cash register reading People *magazine.*

I close the notebook and pocket my pen for now. I'm on my third beer, feeling very tan, sunglasses atop my head. "Excuse me," I say to the woman in the yellow dress.

She looks at me. "Hm?"

"I couldn't help noticing you're almost through with your drink there, and I was wondering…"

"Sure, go ahead. Buy me a drink."

Remaining smooth, I tell the bartender to bring this lady here another pina colada.

She thanks me.

"The name's John, by the way," I tell her.

She tells me hers: Angela.

"That's a very pretty name." I consider adding, *For a very pretty woman*, but that seems a little worn, and anyway she isn't very pretty.

We talk.

She works part-time in an insurance office: Allstate.

"The good hands people," I say, smiling, cupping my hands.

"Mm," she says, nodding, looking rather bored with me already.

I tell her I'm out here from the Chicago area gathering raw material for a screenplay titled *Going Native*, tapping the large red notebook next to my beer.

She laughs, then apologizes and explains that everyone in L.A. is writing a screenplay, don't I know that?

Tapping the notebook harder, I tell her there's a part in here for Bob DeNiro that fits him like a glove.

"*Bob* DeNiro," she says, looking amused. "*Well.*"

"Like a fucking glove," I repeat.

She lowers her head and sips her drink from the little straw.

I lean towards her along the bar: "Tell you a secret. This is part of the movie right here, the two of us talking. In fact, me telling you this secret is part of—"

"I have to go now," she says, standing up.

"Well . . . hey. Finish your drink anyway."

"I have to feed my dog."

"Your *dog*?" I say, showing interest, wanting her to stay and tell me about her dog. "You have a dog, Angela?"

"It's not unusual."

I ask her its name.

"It's . . . Fido," she says.

"That's a very appropriate name for a dog. What kind are we talking about?"

"Big dog," she says. "With huge teeth. Thanks for the drink. "

"*Finish* it why don't ya."

Purse across her shoulder, she wishes me good luck with my screenplay.

I ask her, "Ever done any acting? Because I'll tell ya, there's a part in here would fit you like a—"

"Bye, now." She heads for the door.

"Hey, Angela?"

She turns.

"If your dog ever came after me, know what I would do to him? Do you want to know?"

She sighs and walks out of the bar.

I return to my beer. "I'd gut him like a fucking catfish."

I light a cigarette and set it in the ash tray, open my notebook, pluck the pen from my shirt pocket, and get it all down, about Angela and her sad yellow dress, her pina coladas in the middle of the afternoon, her dreams of movie stardom, and her only real friend in the world, her dog Fido.

I close the notebook. "Yo," I call out, lifting my empty bottle.

Angela's attitude threw me off a little, but now that I've got her in my notebook I'm feeling okay again, feeling pretty good in fact—about my growing screenplay, about the thirty dollars in my wallet, the eight *hundred* dollars in my room, about my suntan, about the night ahead.

The bartender manages to drag himself away from his *People* magazine long enough to bring me another Heinekin.

I compliment him on the beautiful weather out here.

"Thanks," he says.

"Know what it's prob'ly doing in *Chicago* right now? As we speak?"

"No idea."

"*Snowing*. Wind-chill factor, twenty below." I give a laugh. "Worst weather in the world." I raise my hand to God. "Literally. In the *world*."

"You might be right." He takes the empty bottle and drags his bored, weary ass back to the register.

"I *might* be right? I'm *from* there, okay? Suburb, any-way."

"How 'bout that," he says.

"Yeah, how 'bout that. Born and raised, pal."

He opens his *People* magazine again.

"'City of the big shoulders,'" I quote. "Ever hear that? It's from a poem by Carl Sandburg, called 'Chicago.'" I try to remember some more of it, but I can't, and take a drink. I ask him if he's aware that Chicago has the tallest build-ing in the world. I raise my hand to God: "Literally. In the world."

He nods, continues reading.

This fucking guy.

"Tell you something else we got," I say to him. "The best damn *people* in the world."

He turns a page, without comment.

"*Nice* people. Friendly. Know what I mean? Always a smile and a big hello: 'Hey there, how ya doin'? How 'bout those Cubbies?'"

He goes on reading.

"Those Cubbies," I say quietly, looking off, my eyes filling up. And I can't help it, I start singing, not very loud at all: "'Myyy kind of town, Chicago is, my kind of town, Chicago is, my kind of people too, people who—'"

"Hey."

I stop.

He stares at me for a long, hard-assed moment, then returns to his magazine.

I sit there nodding at him: *Fine. Have it your way, pal.* I pluck the pen from my pocket, open the notebook and get it all down:

JACK (singing quietly, with deep feeling): My kind of town, Chicago is my kind of town . . .

BARTENDER: Hey, you. Shut the fuck up.

JACK (singing louder): Chicago is my kind of people too . . .

BARTENDER (crosses to him): Hear what I said, buddy?

JACK: People who smile at you and eeeeach time I roam . . .

BARTENDER (pointing finger in Jack's face): I'm warning you, pal.

JACK: Chicago is calling me home, Chicago is . . .

BARTENDER (pulling out a pistol from under the bar): Does this make things any clearer?

JACK: *The Wrigley Building, Chicago is . . .*

BARTENDER *(cocks gun): You gonna stop?*

JACK: *The Union Station, Chicago is . . .*

BARTENDER: *Three . . . two . . .*

JACK: *One town that won't let you down . . .*

BARTENDER *(lowering gun, nodding in admiration): You got guts, mister. I'll give ya that.*

BOTH *(singing together): It's myyy kiiind of town!*

(They laugh and embrace, not sexually. Fast fade.)

I close the notebook. He's still reading his magazine. "Yo," I call out amiably, waving my empty bottle, giving him another chance.

MIRACLE IN THE RAIN

Hi Cheryl,

How you doing? Hey, it's really something out here—palm trees, incredible weather, everyone on roller skates. I was wondering, could you send me some money so I can get home? I don't want to ask Dad.

The truth is, I didn't do very good out here. Mostly, all I did was sit around in bars trying to write a screenplay about a guy who mostly sits around in bars trying to write a screenplay. I didn't even see any movie stars. The closest I came was some old woman getting out of a cab yesterday who looked like she might be Jane Wyman. I had just watched Miracle in the Rain *that morning in my room—I've got this room with a bed and television, bathroom down the hall—and I yelled out to her, "Jane, you were great!" I wasn't even drunk. Ever see that movie, Cheryl? Her soldier boyfriend, Van Johnson, gets killed in action and it's all pretty sappy, but there's this one scene where she's standing on a little bridge in the park, looking around at the trees and the people, a beautiful day, but she just keeps shaking her head, amazed at how empty the world is, how utterly fucking desolate. "I can't stand it," she says in that soft little voice. "I just can't stand it," she says.*

Anyway, turned out it wasn't her getting out of the cab, just some old woman. Which is what I hate about L.A., thinking someone getting out of a cab who looks like Jane Wyman is either really Jane Wyman or just some old woman.

Could you send me, say, fifty? A hundred? I don't know, you decide. Feel free. Thanks, Cheryl. For everything.

Love, John

RAGING BULL

I took my dad to see it, a middle-of-the-week, late-after-noon matinee at the River Oaks Mall. I was back living at home—just for a while, I promised, just until I could save a little—and he was recently retired after cutting meat at Novak's Butcher Shop for forty-five years. It was odd and a little disturbing to see him home during a weekday, find-ing little jobs for himself.

"I'm gonna go see a movie," I told him. "Wanna come?"

"Nah, go ahead. I gotta take care of this sink."

He never had much use for movies, for sitting down that long watching make-believe life, when there was already real life. The only actor's name he knew was Bette Davis. If you were watching a movie on TV, he might stand there in the doorway for a moment and ask if that was Bette Davis.

"No, that's Joanne Woodward."

"Looks like Bette Davis," he would say, and go back to whatever he was working on: a stopped-up sink, a faulty door latch, a shorted lamp, a leaky shower head . . .

But here was a movie about a boxer, a real one, an *Italian* one, from the days when he and Mike and I would sit together on the couch watching the *Friday Night Fights*, brought to you by Gillette Razor Blades: "How're ya fixed for blades?" The bell would ring and a guy in white trunks and a guy in black trunks would come out and start circling each another, peeking over their gloves, Dad telling them, "C'mon, throw a punch, for Christ sake," Mike and I saying, "Hit 'im, *hit* 'im." And once they finally started hitting each another we'd be quiet and still.

My mother disapproved of boxing: "Watching two idiots beat the shit out of each other."

"It's a *skill*," Dad would explain to her.

He always told us, "Keep moving in and keep your hands up, hit him and cover up, hit him and cover up, like that, see?"

Back then, I was always getting into fights and losing because I never actually punched the other guy, preferring to wrestle him down, but the other guy was never squeamish about punching *me*, and when I'd been punched enough times to justify going down I would do so, and stay there.

"It's a movie about Jake LaMotta, Dad," I told him now.

"Oh?"

"It's supposed to be pretty good."

"Yeah?"

"Pretty true-to-life."

"All right, let's go see." He put his tools away.

Driving there, I told him, "This guy Robert DeNiro who plays him, he's a pretty good movie actor."

"So it's not really him."

"LaMotta? No, it's *about* him, but there's an actor who's . . . you know . . ."

"Pretending."

"Right. But he's good."

"The actor."

"He's *very* good."

"So you already seen this."

"No, I'm just saying, he's a good actor, from other movies."

"You like him, huh?"

"I don't *like* him, I'm just saying."

"Good actor."

"That's all I'm saying."

"Hey, whoa, it's thirty-five along here."

I slowed down.

He paid for the tickets, amazed at the price. "Holy Christ," he told the girl, who shrugged.

We went in and found seats. And I must say, it felt very peculiar sitting in a movie theater next to Dad. He sat straight, his big crooked fingers on his knees, waiting politely for the screen to come to life. I hoped and prayed there wouldn't be any nudity.

The lights went down.

I liked the opening a lot, during the credits: DeNiro alone in the ring, from a smoky distance, shadow boxing in slow motion, this beautiful, sad operatic music playing.

But once the movie started I could sense my father stiffen up, resistant, having never heard the word "fuck" in a movie before:

—*Joey, you gotta talk to your fuckin' brother.*

—*You talk to him.*

—*I can't talk to him, he don't like me.*

—*Nobody fuckin' likes you.*

—*Talk to him, will ya?*

—*Hey, Sal?*

—*What.*

—*Go fuck yourself.*

But just when I was thinking what a huge mistake this was, Dad very quietly chuckled. Someone had called someone a *gumbadi*, Italian for *pal*, a word from the old neighborhood: southside Chicago, tomato gardens, Freddy Nudo's Tap, cigar smoke, boxing, the horses, bookies, his bowling team. We had an eight-by-eleven of the team, in their Nudo's Tap shirts: Joe Chiapetti, Eddie Munno, Lou Paparelli, Jimmy Rossi, my dad and Uncle Gene: gumbadis.

But then LaMotta meets the beautiful Vickie and I got worried. Then sure enough, pretty soon they're in bed and she's slowly kissing him all down his stomach.

I didn't know what to do. I wanted to get out of there, pretend I had to use the bathroom, but that wouldn't look good, like I had to go beat off, so I sat there very still, but I didn't want to be sitting there *too* still, like I was mesmerized, and yet at the same time I didn't want to fidget, like I was getting worked up, although I certainly didn't want to convey indifference, give a big yawn or something. Meanwhile, I had no idea what was going on with Dad, if he was wondering what the hell kind of dirty movie I'd brought him to, or was he embarrassed like me, or morally outraged, or possibly—who knows?—thoroughly enjoying this, or even possibly feeling rather sad, like he'd missed the boat. I had no idea.

Vickie, meanwhile, keeps slowly working her way down, with an occasional shot of DeNiro's complicated expression, and then at the last moment he stops her: "I gotta fight Robinson tomorrow. I can't fool around."

And what a huge relief the immediate next scene was, back in the ring, LaMotta versus Sugar Ray Robinson, the familiar voice of radio announcer Don Dunphy, and the clean, hard steady passionate blows, Dad and I both sitting up straighter, fresh air filling our lungs.

In most fight movies you're pulling for the main character, and that's how this one worked for a while. But then LaMotta starts beating up on people outside the ring, including Vickie, including his loyal brother Joey, and, by the end of the movie, he's a fat slob beating his own head against a wall.

Alone, I probably would have considered the movie some kind of grim masterpiece, a profound study of violence, something like that. But being with Dad I found myself wondering what's the point of paying good money to see a movie if it doesn't have a happy ending.

Walking to the car, I asked him what he thought.

"I don't like that kinda language. That shouldn't be allowed."

I asked him what he thought of the movie otherwise.

He shook his head. "Dumb dago."

But on the way home he said nice things about LaMotta in the ring: "He didn't do a lotta dancing around. He came to fight, he came *after* you."

I said I thought Robert DeNiro did a pretty good job in the fight scenes.

"You like that guy, huh?"

"I don't *like* him, Dad. I'm just saying."

"Hey, thirty-five along here."

I slowed down.

COMING HOME

I didn't want to talk about the movie, but she was limp from it. That was how she put it. "I'm actually, literally *limp*," she said, going limp all over to show me.

"I know what you mean," I told her.

"Do you?"

"Limp, yeah."

We were sitting in a booth in Alf's, me with a beer, her with a bloody mary, our first time out together, both of us trying hard. But I didn't want to talk about the movie—Jon Voight coming back from Vietnam paralyzed in a wheelchair, Bruce Dern returning so disillusioned he ends up drowning himself, and all I ever got was some teargas in my eyes once at a campus peace rally.

I told her if she wanted to see a *really* good Jon Voight movie, she ought to see *Midnight Cowboy*. "Ever see that?"

"No, as a matter of fact I never have. I've heard it's very excellent."

"'Talk about limp, you'd be a wet noodle.'"

She laughed, a little too loud.

Her name was Jill. She worked in Payroll at the city college where I'd found a tutoring spot. I thought my first check was a misprint and when I came to complain, she was quite nice about it, showing me there was no mistake, the decimal point was where it belonged. She had a very pleasant freckled face and she wasn't all *that* fat, not really, so I went ahead and asked her out. And here we were. She looked very nice in her shiny green dress.

"I thought Jane *Fonda* was awfully good," she said, "didn't you?"

"Very much so," I told her, "yes. But I'll tell you something, did you ever see her in *Klute*?"

"Is that with Donald Sutherland?"

"There you go."

"I *saw* that, yes, you're right, she was good in that. Excellent, in fact."

"Terrific actress," I said. "Top notch."

"And so pretty," she added.

"You kidding? She's beautiful. Just a . . . remarkably beautiful woman. Breathtaking, in fact."

"Okay, *okay*," she said, laughing. "I get it. Point taken."

"No, I was just, you know, agreeing."

"*I'll* say." She began vigorously stirring her drink with the little plastic straw. "Sounds to me like somebody's in love."

I laughed it off. "Right," I said, "me and Jane," and sipped my beer.

"I don't blame you," she said, still stirring her drink. "She *is* beautiful. Very slender, very—"

"Her *father* was a damn good actor," I said.

"'Breathtaking,' as you put it."

"Henry Fonda?"

She looked up from her drink. "Jane." She was definitely angry, you could see.

I asked about her drink. "How *is* that, by the way."

"I haven't tried it yet."

"I know," I said.

She cocked her head, smiling, blinking. "So why did you ask?"

"Just, you know, trying to encourage you."

"To get drunk?"

"No. God."

She started poking at the ice now, looking down at it. "She was a big peace activist, you know."

Still on Jane.

"That's true," I said. "Yes."

"Quite the radical," she added.

"*Very* political," I agreed. "By the way, want to know a really good political movie? I saw it the other night on TV. It's pretty old, with Broderick Crawford—"

"If I was a guy?" she said. "Over there? During Vietnam? And I heard about this woman, this . . . *actress*? Siding with the enemy?"

"Oh, I don't think she actually—"

"I would hate her. I don't care *how* slender and breathtaking she is, I would hate . . . her . . . guts."

I was wishing I hadn't used the word "breathtaking."

Then she asked me, point blank, "Were *you* over there?"

I was afraid of this. "Vietnam, you mean?"

"Did you serve?"

"Well . . . actually, Jill? To be perfectly honest?"

"I didn't think so," she said.

Which pissed me off. "What I was going to *say* . . ."

She waited.

"I was going to *say*, I don't feel very much like talking about it, all right? If you don't mind?"

She was studying me.

"I mean, *you* saw the movie," I added, letting her take that any way she wanted.

She nodded, sympathetically it seemed.

I sipped my beer. Then, trying to move us along, I held up the glass, studying it. "This is very good, by the way. It's German, you know. Has a nice bite to it, a nice bitterness. Which I like. I like that in a beer."

"Bitterness?"

"Oh, absolutely," I said, and took another drink: "Ahhh."

"Is that because you're a bitter person?" she asked.

"Must be," I said, just kidding.

She looked down at her drink, stirring it slowly. "Did you lose a lot of buddies over there?"

Aw, Jesus, I thought.

But then right away she said, "I'm sorry. You don't want to talk about it."

I thanked her.

We sat there. I was looking down into my glass trying to think of something non-Vietnam to talk about. Then she suddenly leaned forward, reached across the table and laid her hand over mine. "Please let me help?" she said, looking into my eyes. "I want to, very much. Will you let me? Please?"

Carefully I slid my hand out from under hers and placed it in my lap along with the other one. Then I drew a long, truth-telling breath. "Jill, listen to me."

"That's all right," she said, sitting back. "You don't have to explain. We don't even know each other and here I am, trying to . . . *heal* you. Blame it on the movie. I was trying to be like—what was her name? The Jane Fonda character?"

"Sally, I think."

"I was trying to be like Sally, an overweight Sally. Fat Sal."

"Hey, cut it out," I said. "You're not that fat."

She laughed. "'Not that fat.' I like that. Thank you very much." She started poking at the ice in her drink again.

"No, I mean it."

"Did you have a girlfriend over there?" she asked. "One of those cute little brown little tiny petite little—"

"Listen to me, Jill. Will you? Please?"

"I'll stop now," she promised. There were tears in her eyes. She looked in her purse for a tissue but couldn't find one. "Do you have a handkerchief?"

"Actually . . ."

"Never mind." She used a napkin.

While she was blowing her nose I told her I wasn't over there.

She stopped.

"I wasn't even in the military," I said. "I wasn't drafted and I didn't enlist."

She was staring at me, still holding the napkin to her nose.

"I was a hippie, Jill. A longhaired, potsmoking hippie, hollering out with all the other hippies, 'Hell no, we won't go.'"

She nodded, slowly.

I told her, "I'm very sorry I misled you. It was a disgusting thing to do and I apologize."

Still nodding, she said quietly, "I've heard about this. I've heard about guys doing this."

"Pretending they were in Vietnam?"

"Pretending they *weren't*."

Oh, Lord.

"And not just to others," she added, leaning forward, "but to themselves."

"Jill, I wasn't there."

"Total, complete denial." She started reaching for my hand again.

I put it back in my lap. "Look in my file," I told her. "Payroll has my resume, right? My job history?"

"They should."

"Monday morning take a look, see what it says. See if there's anything about Vietnam, or the military, ever."

That gave her pause, you could see.

"I wasn't a soldier, Jill."

She cocked her head, studying me.

"I'm sorry, I just wasn't," I said, and sipped my beer.

She gave a sad little smile. "Actually? Now that I think about it? It's kind of hard to imagine you in a helmet, holding a rifle. No offense, but it's kind of difficult to picture."

"Is that right."

"No offense."

"None taken," I assured her. "You think I'm ashamed?"

"Probably not."

"But you think I should be."

She shrugged.

"Let me ask you something," I said. "Just curious, okay?"

"Go ahead."

"Have you ever been gassed?"

"Like at the dentist, you mean?"

"I'm talking about teargas. Have you ever been teargassed, Jill?"

"Not to my knowledge."

"Yeah well, you would know, trust me. I thought I was blinded. I actually thought I was never going to see again. Do you know what that's like? To think you're never going to see again?"

"Were you crying?"

"No, I was not. I had *tears*, but that was from the gas."

"So where was this?"

"Northern Illinois University, fall of seventy-one."

"What, a sit-in or something?"

"Whatever. I'm just saying, okay? I was *out* there."

She gave that little smile again. "In the trenches?"

"So to speak."

"You and Jane?"

"Go ahead and laugh. But you know what? We stopped the war, Jill. We stopped the carnage. 'Enough,' we said." I leaned forward and poked the table with each word: "'This, will, not, do.'"

She spoke quietly. "Could you sit back please?"

"Sorry." I sat back.

I drank from my beer. And she, finally, drank from her bloody mary, taking a brief pull on the little straw—and made a face.

"No good?" I said.

"Too much black pepper."

"You're kidding."

"Why would I kid?"

"You want me to complain? I *will*, believe me." I felt like making a huge stink. "I don't mean to scare you, Jill, but I don't put *up* with this kind of bullshit."

"Black pepper?"

"Whatever. I don't put *up* with it."

"That's all right."

"No, Jill, It's *not*," I told her, and stood up. "I'm sorry but this *will* . . . *not* . . . *do*."

"John . . ." That was the first time all evening she'd said my name. She said it rather sadly, looking up at me. "Sit down, okay? Will you? Please?"

I sat down.

She thanked me.

We sat there.

I asked her—calmly, quietly—if she would like me to order another bloody mary, one with less black pepper in it.

She didn't think so.

We sat there some more.

I made a final effort to somehow get the evening back on track: "Mark my words," I told her, tapping the table: "Best actor: Jon Voight, *Coming Home*. You heard it here."

She nodded. "I'll remember," she promised, then looked at her watch: "Oh, my."

ONE FLEW OVER THE CUCKOO'S NEST

Elizabeth M. Callahan
English 101
Room 318
Mr. Manderino

<u>*"The Combine" as the Novel's Central Metaphor*</u>

Mr. Manderino, I am very sorry but I do not know what you are even talking about. The Combine? What is that? You say Chief Broom mentions it a lot? Excuse me, but Chief Broom doesn't even <u>speak</u>. In fact everyone thinks he is totally deaf and dumb until late in the movie when Jack Nicholson gives him a stick of gum and he says, "Mmm, Juicy Fruit," and Jack Nicholson practically falls right out of his chair!

So I guess it must be only in the <u>book</u> where he talks about The Combine as a Central Metaphor, although I have to say, it's a little hard to imagine Chief Broom all of a sudden talking like an English teacher! But I will take your word for it because no, I did not read the book, and yes, I know you said we couldn't just rent the movie, but Mr. Manderino I am a single mother with a four-year-old daughter and a full-time job and I am very sorry but I don't always have <u>time</u> to sit down and read an entire book, and if the movie is <u>based</u> on the book and if that same movie just happened to win five Academy Awards for that year, including Best Picture, then, with all due respect, I really do not see the problem.

Have you ever seen it? I'm sure you probably have, probably more than once, if you were honest. But in case you haven't, it stars Jack Nicholson as the ever-rambunctious roustabout Randle McMurphy, forever trying to get the other patients to lighten up and enjoy life, and ending up as a vegetable, a cruel and unusual fate for one so full of fun and mischief, but I guess the message is, that's what happens to the individual in modern society nowadays who dares to be free, free at last, thank God almighty, free at last.

In conclusion, let me just say I am very disappointed in you, Mr. Manderino. You come on like Mister Laidback, Mister Nice Guy, in your jeans and your loose-fitting sweaters, talking like you just got back from Woodstock, then you stab us in the back with your Combine as a Central Metaphor. I honestly thought you were on <u>our</u> side.

Also, by the way, just thought you should know. If I flunk this class? I will lose my financial aid. And if that happens? I will have to drop out of school. And if <u>that</u> happens? I will be stuck forever at Bonanza and my four-year-old daughter will be doomed to a cheap, crappy, discount existence.

"Mommy, why do I have to wear clothes from Goodwill? Why can't I ever have anything nice?"

"Hush, little one, don't cry. It's because of The Combine as a Central Metaphor."

GANDHI

I lived for a while in the basement of a middle-aged couple from Bombay. I liked it down there. The walls and floor were cool cement, I had a corduroy couch that opened into a bed, a little black and white TV, some carpet samples for throw rugs, and everything had the smell of sandalwood incense clinging to it.

The husband's name was Ruki: tall, bald, brown as an acorn and very amiable. I didn't care much for his tiny wife, though. Maha had a red dot in the middle of her forehead and a sharp ugly voice. I could hear her up there:

"Ruki, how many times must I tell you?"

"Ruki, I am losing my patience!"

"Ruki, bring me a glass of water!"

"Ruki!"

He often came downstairs, heavily, and sat with me on the couch. Sometimes we watched television. Or he would talk. One evening he told me if you climbed the Himalayas

high enough, here and there you would find solitary blissful men sitting cross-legged in the snow wearing nothing
but a loin cloth.

"With little spinning wheels?"

"Are you making fun?"

"I'm sorry. Not at all."

"You're thinking of Gandhi perhaps?"

I told him I'd seen the movie when it came out last year.
"With what's his name . . . British actor . . . excellent . . ."

"I met him once."

"No kidding? I think he won an Oscar for it. What's his
name again?"

"Not your actor. Gandhi himself. I was very small, of
course, a mere infant. What a kind face he had."

"Ruki!" Maha called down.

"Yes, my cherished one!" He stood. "Excuse me please,"
he said, and began heading up the stairs. But then he suddenly turned back and said he'd forgotten to ask: "How
does one go about applying for the Peace Corps?"

"The Peace Corps?"

"Yes please."

"Well . . . I'm not real sure. Any particular country?"

"Ruki! I am waiting!"

"No particular country."

As part of my rent agreement, I was allowed to use a
shelf in their refrigerator up there, which was all I needed
for my beer, bread and baloney. I remember one Saturday
afternoon I came up for a beer as Maha was sweeping the

kitchen floor and Ruki was out mowing the lawn. "Ruki has left some of his tea," she said. "You may finish it." She was standing near the sink, holding out the cup, smiling benevolently. "Otherwise I will throw it down the drain."

I laughed. I couldn't help it.

"Have I said something amusing?"

"Yes," I told her, yanking a can of beer from its plastic noose.

"Please explain."

I walked over, took the cup from her hand, dumped the tea into the sink and gave her back the cup.

She stood there studying me, her head to one side. "You are very dynamic," she observed.

"What can I say?" I popped open my beer and headed downstairs to watch the rest of the Cubs game.

When his Peace Corps application arrived, Ruki came downstairs with it, excited. But not only was he rather old for a volunteer, he lacked any useful skills. And yet he felt certain there must be *something* he could do, somewhere in the world, preferably in a supervisory capacity. "For example, I could oversee the construction of a bridge across a narrow but very treacherous river."

I pointed out he had no training or experience as an engineer.

He admitted this was true, but said he could nevertheless very easily imagine himself inspiring a group of young volunteers to build a bridge which would not only span a river but would also span religious, racial and cultural differences as well. "For, as you know, we are all brothers," he said.

"I suppose."

He looked through the application. "They ask here for a personal reference. Would you be so kind?"

I told him I'd be glad to write something.

"I am in your debt. May I ask—I am curious—what will you say?"

"Well . . ."

"Please be candid."

"I'll say Ruki is a good man."

"You are very kind."

"I'll say . . . he's an intelligent man."

"I am blushing. Please continue."

"Let's see, he's a very . . . a very . . ."

"Happy man?"

I looked at him. "Okay. Sure. I'll say that."

"You seem doubtful."

"Not at all."

"Perhaps you could mention my having once met Gandhi, do you suppose?"

"Well . . ."

"Mention how he took my little hand in his and said, 'Ruki, listen to me. I am going to tell you something you must never forget.'"

"*Ruki*," Maha called down, "come here please."

He sighed, gathered up his papers.

"Well?" I asked. "What did Gandhi say?"

He sat there for a moment looking off, then shrugged. "It's of no importance."

"'All through history,'" I quoted, "'the way of truth has always won.'"

He looked at me. "Is that from your movie?"

"Well, yeah, but I'm sure he actually said it."

"I touched his *hand*."

"I know, Ruki. I know."

"You know. What do you know? Nothing. *Movies*. That's all you know. I touched his—"

"Ruki, I am waiting!"

"Yes!" he shouted angrily, and got up from the couch. "I am on my way!" He headed up the stairs. But then he stopped and hurried down again. "I am so sorry. Please forgive my words."

They had hurt me—it surprised me how deeply—but I nodded, holding up my hand, and told him not to worry about it.

"You will write the letter?" he asked quietly.

"Yes," I assured him.

"You are very kind." He quickly headed up the stairs again.

APOCALYPSE NOW

American helicopter gunships come swarming over the little Vietnamese village, people in coolie hats—men, women and children—running for their lives, Wagner's "The Flight of the Valkyries" blaring. It's horrible and appalling, but thrilling too, with that music.

Afterwards, as Robert Duvall is striding around in a cavalry hat barking orders, my brother Mike hits the Pause button on the remote. "Right back," he says, and hurries off, leaving Robert Duvall standing there with his hands on his hips.

This is the third time Mike has checked on Joey since the movie started. His wife Debbie is away, something with her job, so he's a little nervous, Joey being only eight months old, and I understand, I don't blame him, but I rented this to show him what I regard as one of the greatest war movies ever made, and all this stopping and starting is destroying the rhythm of it.

I reach over and grab the remote.

"You want anything?" he calls out from the kitchen.

"No, I'm good. Let's go, amigo."

He returns with a can of Coke. "You should see him *now*, he's all curled up in the corner, his little fists like this."

"Joe Palooka. Okay, ready?"

"Gimme that thing."

"Here we go." I hit Play.

Martin Sheen and his little crew are soon back in their patrol boat, resuming their journey down the river, deeper and deeper into the jungle, their mission to find and kill Colonel Kurtz, this decorated Green Beret who's gone all the way down the river and around the bend, who, in fact, has gone quite completely insane.

Spooky, hypnotic music is playing.

I can feel Mike getting pulled in, feel his stillness at the other end of the couch, so I keep quiet, letting the movie speak for itself.

It's night when the boat finally passes Do Lung Bridge, the last army outpost. *Beyond it*, Martin Sheen tells us, *there was only Kurtz*.

"Stop, okay?"

"Ah, Jesus." I hit Pause.

"Sorry," he says, hurrying off.

I take a drink from his Coke. On the screen there's a view from the back of the boat, the brown churning wake, the lights of the bridge in the distance, the boat entering uncharted waters now, literally and of course metaphorically.

"He's really sweating," Mike says, returning. "The back of his hair's all stuck to his neck. I took the blanket off him."

"Babies tend to sweat quite a lot in their sleep," I assure him.

"You making that up?"

"I think I read it somewhere. Ready?"

"Yeah, I guess."

"He's fine, Mike."

"Go ahead. I want to meet this Kurtz."

"You will," I tell him ominously, and hit Play.

"It's Marlon Brando, right?"

"Shh."

A heavy fog is on the river the following morning and as they move slowly through it, there's suddenly an attack from the invisible shore—with spears and arrows, as if they're not only passing deeper into the jungle but deeper into human history, towards some Primordial Origin. I consider hitting Pause to briefly explain this "heart-of-darkness" theme at work, from the Conrad novel, but I don't want to break the spell.

They continue down the brown, meandering river.

He was close, says Martin Sheen. *I couldn't see him yet, but I could feel him.* A slow, steady bass note begins thudding, like a beating heart, Mike and I sitting very quiet, very still . . .

Then Joey starts wailing.

Mike is up and gone without a word.

I hit Pause.

167

Apparently you can't ever have it. You can't ever have a perfect movie moment. It's like a fucking law. You can't have it. And why? Because there's always something. Always.

Paused, Martin Sheen is standing at the front of the boat looking through binoculars. I know what he's seeing. They're approaching the Kurtz compound and he's looking at dead naked bodies hanging from the trees, at piles of skulls along the shore, at huge stone idols. He's soon going to meet squirrely Dennis Hopper, who will take him to Kurtz—massive, baldheaded Marlon Brando—and after Martin Sheen finally hacks him up with a machete, Brando will lie there staring straight up, whispering, *The . . . horror. The . . . horror.*

Mike returns holding Joey, who's quiet now. "Joe, look who's here."

I tell him hi and ask Mike, "So now what?"

"Go ahead," he says, standing there jiggling him a little. "Hit it."

"You're not gonna put him back?"

"He'll just start crying again."

"What if we close the door and turn up the volume?"

"That's . . . not a good idea."

"There's only about forty minutes left."

"He'll be quiet. Won't you, Joe."

His head against his father's chest, Joey is looking at me out of one suspicious eye.

I get up from the couch. "Tell you what. Leave the tape in the machine. We'll watch the rest some other night." I grab my jacket from the chair. "Or go ahead and watch it yourself, I don't care."

"What's the problem? He'll be quiet. Look at him."

"I can't watch a movie with a baby in the room, okay? I'm sorry. I can't do it. I won't."

"Joe, tell him."

"Tell me what."

"You're being goofy."

"Yeah, well, what can I say." I walk up and bring my face close to Joey's. "Nice seeing you, Joe. Always a treat."

He gives a whimper and buries his face in his father's golf shirt.

I look at Mike. "What the hell is *that*?"

"I don't know," Mike says, looking down at him. "Maybe he thinks you don't like him." He goes walking him around, Joey peering over his father's shoulder, keeping an eye on me.

So now I feel like a real asshole.

"What're you talking about?" I say, following them, addressing Joey. "Did I say I didn't like you? Did I say that, Joe? Did I?"

Joey ducks back down.

"Joe," Mike tells him, turning to me. "It's your uncle John. He wants to talk. He wants to apologize."

"I wouldn't go *that* far. Here, lemme have him for a minute."

"What for?"

"I'm not gonna hurt him. Jesus."

"All right but if he starts screaming . . ."

"You'll get him back, believe me."

"Joe, wanna see Uncle John? Here, go see Uncle John. You're okay," he tells him, carefully handing him over, "you're okay," Joey looking too scared to cry out. I hold him by the armpits, face to face. He doesn't squirm or kick, just hangs there staring at me, bug-eyed.

The . . . horror.

"Listen to me, Joe. Listen carefully. You are not in danger. Do you understand? I have no intention of—"

"*Hold* him," Mike tells me.

"Right." I bring him carefully against my chest, left arm under his diapered butt, right hand on the back of his sweaty little T-shirt. He still hasn't screamed but he's ready to, all clenched up, breathing fast and shallow. "Re*lax*, will ya? I'm your uncle, for Christ sake."

"Walk him around."

I do so, patting him on the back, telling him not to be afraid, that I'm not a monster, we've all got our faults, our dark places, mentioning Colonel Kurtz from the movie he ruined, explaining there's a bit of Kurtz in all of us, some of that same heart of darkness, which by the way, I tell him, was the book they used, *Heart of Darkness* by Joseph Conrad, written long before Vietnam of course, around nineteen hundred, nineteen-oh-five, somewhere in there—then suddenly Joey does this wonderful thing, he gives a gigantic yawn.

I look over at Mike. "See that?"

"I did," he says, nodding, as pleased as me.

I walk Joey around some more, telling him how wonderful he is, what a wonderful little boy, while he actually falls asleep in my arms.

FIELD OF DREAMS

Kevin Costner keeps telling his wife and little girl all about Shoeless Joe Jackson, what a great ballplayer he was, quoting batting statistics, quoting Babe Ruth who called him the greatest hitter he ever saw, and then when Shoeless Joe finally appears—his ghost or whatever—they've got him batting right-handed.

I whispered to Nan, "He was a *left*-handed batter."

She nodded.

"He *threw* right-handed but he batted *lefty*."

She patted my leg.

I sat back and folded my arms.

The movie was obviously intended to be very magical and moving and maybe it was—people were sniffling, including Nan at a couple places—and the ending was clearly designed to bring tears, Kevin Costner playing catch with his dead father, the music working away.

His father's glove looked a lot like my dad's.

He used to play catch with me and Mike in the alley, in the twilight, home from the butcher shop, still in his tie, tossing us pop-ups and grounders and a flutterball that didn't really flutter, wearing this plump little old-time glove—no web, no lacing between the fingers—a Spalding, Dazzy Vance model. He'd had that glove since he was a kid, our age. He kept it oiled, up in his closet.

I took it to the park one day, just to see. You had to catch the ball right in the pocket, with two hands, no fancy stuff. I felt like one of those gritty old Tinkers-to-Evers-to-Chance type guys. But then I muffed an easy grounder and went back to my own glove, a Wilson, Eddie Matthews.

And that was the only one I came home with.

By the time I remembered and raced back, it was gone. I looked all over the ball field, twice, then all around the entire darkening park: the other ball diamond, the football field, the playground area.

It was gone.

I asked around the next day but no one knew anything: "Probably starlings," was the general opinion. Ever since the previous summer's starling crisis, they were blamed for anything missing, even things like bicycles.

"A little catch?" Dad offered one evening not long afterwards.

Mike and I glanced at each other. "Sure," we said. "Okay."

And when his glove wasn't in the closet I swore we didn't know where it was, which was true enough. So then we pretended to help him look for it—in the other closets, down in the basement, out in the garage, where he finally turned to us: "What'd you guys do, take it somewhere and leave it?"

Mike looked down. I gave a bewildered look, like Dad was speaking Italian.

He waited.

Then I looked down, too.

He sighed. "Nice going," he said quietly, and went back in the house.

Dad never hit us, either one of us, ever, but there were times when I almost wished he would.

I told Mike, "We're gonna find that glove."

"Think so?"

We grew up, went off to college, got jobs, all that, but whenever I saw a table at a yard sale or a flea market with an old chubby-fingered ball glove among the dirty vases and cracked dolls, my heart would give a foolish little leap and I'd go over and see if it was a Spalding, Dazzy Vance model. It never was.

Then one day Mike phoned and told me Dad had dropped dead that morning in the bathroom.

Kevin Costner's dead father comes back and they play catch together in a soft golden light, the music tugging and yanking away. But I sat there dry-eyed, arms folded, refusing to cry at a movie that can't even get it right about which side of the goddam plate Joe Jackson batted from.

"What bullshit," I told Nan in the lobby afterwards, loud, letting everyone hear. "What a bunch of total, absolute bullshit!"

She got me out of there.

A STREETCAR NAMED DESIRE

—Hello?

—Just me.

—Ma. Hey. What's up?

—I won't keep you. You're probably busy, I know.

—Nah.

—Saw something you might be interested in, that's all.

—Yeah?

—You're sure you're not busy?

—Just grading papers. Go ahead.

—You sure?

—Ma, what is it you wanted.

—Hey.

—What.

—Don't take that tone with me.

—Sorry. Can you tell me, though?

—Tell you what?

—Why you called.

—Never mind. Nothing important.

—Ma . . .

—I'll try some other time when you're in a better—

—Wait. Ma? Y'there? Hey.

—Still here.

—Why did you call?

—I need a reason?

—No. But you said you had one.

—I do. What time is it?

—That's why you called?

—I've got something in the oven—something *you* might be interested in, by the way.

—Oh?

—What time is it?

—It's . . . two-forty.

—All right. The reason I called. I don't usually watch television in the afternoon. I don't like the feeling. I usually read or find something to do. But today I just felt like what's the use, what the hell's the use, why even try.

—Bad day?

—It'll be two years next month. Two years. And yes, I know what you're going to say, "Time heals all wounds."

—I wasn't going to say that.

—"We all have to go some—"

—Or that either.

—"You had fifty-five years with the man."

—Or that.

—And you're right, but you know what? I hate to say it but it doesn't help, not a bit. I'm sorry. I know you mean well.

—Did you want some company?

—No, no. I'm fine. Really. You've got work to do. Papers to grade, right?

—I can bring them over.

—That's not why I called.

—I know. But I'm saying—

—I happened to be looking through the *TV Guide* and saw something on this afternoon I thought you'd probably want to watch, that's all.

—Oh?

—*A Streetcar Named Desire*. Says here . . . let me find it . . . here it is: "Grim, powerful Tennessee Williams drama about a faded Southern belle. Vivien Leigh and Marlon Brando." Four stars they give it. Not that *that* means anything, I've seen some four-star crapola, believe me. But I know how much you like all that Tennessee Williams-type stuff, so I thought I'd let you know. It's on at, let me see, four o'clock.

—Well, thanks. I've seen it but thanks.

—I *figured* you'd seen it but I just thought maybe you'd want to see it again. I know with certain movies I like, things like *Shop Around the Corner*, or *Meet Me in St. Louis*, upbeat things like that, things that make you feel *good* instead of miserable, I can watch them over and over, so I just thought maybe you'd want to—

—See it again, right. Well, thanks. I might. I've got a lot of work to do first—

—Papers to grade.

—Right. But yeah, I'll probably take a look. Anyway, thanks.

—She's a Southern belle, is she? Vivien Leigh? A faded Southern belle?

—Right.

—Like in *Gone with the Wind*, only she wasn't faded, she was still quite young in that. I probably told you, probably more than once, I was the very first person in line at its very first showing in Chicago. It was at the—

—Chicago Theater, right.

—Nineteen thirty-nine. Dear God . . .

—Long time ago?

—No. That's just it. Not at all. Until you actually count out the years. Is this the Civil War?

—Is . . . what, Ma.

—This Tennessee Williams thing. It says she's a faded Southern belle.

—Actually, no, it's more like the nineteen forties, early fifties.

—Oh Jesus, of course, with streetcars, what'm I thinking, they didn't have *street*cars in the—oh God, I'm stupid. I'm very, very stupid and I'm very, very depressed and I know I shouldn't say this, especially to one of my children, but sometimes I honestly truly wish to God I was—

—Ma, hey, c'mon, don't, will ya?

—Don't go there?

—Right.

—That's what your brother says. "Ma, don't go there."

—Well, don't. First of all, you're not stupid. You *are* depressed, I'll give you that.

—Thanks. All right, well, I'll let you get back to your—

—Listen, what time did you say the movie was? Four?

—Four o'clock. So that's, let's see, an hour and . . .

—Why don't I try and finish up and I'll come over and watch it there.

—If you'd like. It's up to you.

—All right. Well. I'll see you in a—

—Might have a little surprise for you.

—Oh?

—Little something.

—What.

—I'm not going to *tell* you. It's still in the oven. Mince pie.

—Sounds good.

—With vanilla ice cream.

—Even better.

—Pick some up, on your way. I was thinking we could watch *Jeopardy*, maybe afterwards play some cards, little two-handed rummy.

—What about *Street*car?

—Streetcar . . .

—The movie. *A Streetcar Named*—

—I thought you'd already seen it. Anyway, I don't understand why you'd want to watch something like that in the first place. Life is gloomy *enough*, isn't it?

—I suppose.

—I've read about this Tennessee Williams. Homosexual. Drug addict. Alcoholic. He killed himself, didn't he?

—I don't think so.

—Well, maybe he should have.

—Ma.

—I'm sorry. That wasn't very nice. I just don't have any patience with people who go around feeling sorry for themselves all the time—and I know what you're thinking, kettle calling the pot, but at least I *try* to snap out of it. I don't often succeed but at least I make an effort. People like that don't even try.

—Ma, how do you know—

—They wallow in it, they glory in it, write novels and plays all about how horrible life is, and we're supposed to be what, grateful? "Oh, thank you for reminding me how shitty life is, I almost forgot. I was almost going to be happy there for a minute." Don't laugh. I'm not trying to be funny. I'm very angry. I get very, very angry lately. I don't know if you've noticed.

—Little bit.

—If Tennessee Williams wants to be a miserable alcoholic homosexual drug addict, that's his business, it's a free country, but why should we have to suffer for it? She was so good in *Gone with the Wind*.

—Vivien Leigh?

—Why would she want to be in something like this, something so morbid and dismal.

—Have you seen it?

—I don't have to see it. Faded Southern belle. Probably drinks. Gets all dressed up, nowhere to go. Listens to music. Lonely, lonely, *lonely*. Oh God, John, I'm so—

—Ma, listen, I'm gonna come over *now*, okay? I'll bring my work over.

—Hurry up.

—I'm on my way.

—I'm short of breath.

—Drink a glass of water.

—I'm starting to panic, oh Jesus I'm starting to panic.

—Ma, listen.

—Talk to me, just talk to me, tell me about the movie, about the faded Southern belle, what happens, go on, hurry up, tell me.

—Well she, she visits her sister . . .

—Uh-huh. Her sister. And then?

—Her sister's name is Stella.

—Stella, okay.

—And she's married—Stella—to Marlon Brando—Stanley Kowalski—and he's a, he's a—well, I don't know, he *bowls*, okay?

—Like your father.

—Except he's not like Dad, he's very, I don't know—

—Moody? Your father was never moody. The man worked like a dog for you kids but never complained, not once, never *thought* to complain. Go ahead. He bowls.

—So Blanche—the Vivien Leigh character, Blanche DuBois, French for—

—I had a friend named Blanche. In high school. Blanche
. . . God what was her last name . . .

—You doing better?

—Little bit. Go ahead, though.

—Well, let's see, she stays with Stella.

—Her sister.

—Right. And Stanley doesn't like her.

—Blanche?

—Right. He thinks she's stuck up.

—A Southern belle.

—Exactly. And she is stuck up, but she's also very, you
know . . .

—Lonely?

—Right.

—Miserable?

—Well . . .

—Wants to die?

—She's pretty unhappy, put it that way.

—Faded.

—There you go. Anyway, it goes on like that, and Stanley eventually sort of . . . you know . . .

—Kills her?

—Rapes her.

—Of course.

—So she ends up going crazy and they send for the men
in the white coats, and . . . that's pretty much it, The End.

—What a lovely story.

—As they're taking her away she says, "I have always
depended on the kindness of—"

—Cunningham.

—Sorry?

—Blanche Cunningham. That was my friend's name. Talk about stuck up. Anyway, what do *I* know, they give it four stars—although, like I said, that doesn't necessarily—there's the oven bell, your pie. Pick up some ice cream on your way, if you'd like.

—Vanilla?

—Whatever. I won't eat any. I'm dieting.

—You're not dying, Ma.

—I said I'm *dieting.*

—Oh. All right, well . . . see you in a bit.

—If you feel like it.

TESTAMENT OF LOVE

As far as I know, the only time I've ever been captured on film, or tape anyway, was in my friend Jim Capano's professionally-produced wedding video, titled *Testament of Love*, which I saw one evening at Jim and Janet's, the three of us sitting on their brand new couch, me in the middle. It was grueling, almost two hours, but Jim kept replacing my beer and I kept finding appropriate things to say:

—*What a great shot of the two of you, huh?*

—*Now that is one cute little flower girl.*

—*Boy, Janet, your dad is really tall.*

—*Look . . . at that . . . cake.*

—*Hey, that guy can dance!*

It was finally almost over. The reception-hall band had quit, and at a table full of empty glasses, Janet's burly brother was speaking earnestly to the camera, an arm around his little wife, wishing Jim and Janet "all the happiness in the whole damn world and boy I really mean that."

Then, suddenly, there I was. As her brother talked on, you could see me in the background at the far end of the room, walking across the empty dance floor in my cheap suit, one hand in my pants pocket, the other holding a bottle of beer.

"Oh, my God," I said quietly, deeply moved.

"What's the matter?" Jim asked.

"Nothing. Janet's brother. He's really muscular."

"Yeah, he works out a lot," she said.

I was gone. I had crossed the floor and was gone.

Janet's brother went on some more about what a wonderful couple Jim and Janet were, even their first *names* beginning with the same letter, while I waited for me to walk across the other way. But I didn't come back. I wondered what I was doing. Probably standing somewhere off by myself, out of the way, just me and my beer.

This was turning out to be one of the saddest movies I had ever seen.

At last the tired happy couple stood waving goodbye, everyone cheering, wishing them all the happiness in the whole damn world. Then fade-out, and across the screen in slender letters: *Not The End But The Beginning*.

Nodding, nodding, I got up from the couch with tears in my eyes: "'Not the end but the beginning,' that's really . . . I like that."

Jim and Janet were touched by how touched I was. We hugged and said things, and I got the hell out of there.

FARGO

I dream I'm in a Chinese restaurant in my pajamas at a table by myself, the actor Steve Buscemi pouring ice water into my glass.

—*Would you care to see a menu?* he says.

—*You're Steve Buscemi!* I tell him.

—*Would you care to see a menu?*

—*You were great in Fargo. I love that movie.*

—*Would you care to—*

—*What are you doing waiting tables?*

—*Would you care to see—*

—*Is this a movie?* I whisper. *Are we in a movie? Is this a scene we're doing here?*

—*Would you care to see a menu?*

—*Yes, waiter,* I tell him with a wink, letting him know I know. *I would like very much to see a menu—if it's not too inconvenient,* I add sarcastically.

He walks off.

I take a sip of water, thinking hard: *Chinese restaurant . . . in my pajamas . . . Steve Buscemi . . .*

It all adds up.

He returns with a menu but I tell him to forget it, I know what's going on: *This isn't a movie, this is a dream!*

He hands me the menu. *I'll be back to take your order,* he says, and walks off again.

I look at the menu. It's in Chinese. But I'm somehow reading it: *Soon . . . you will give . . . a small . . . laugh.*

I can read Chinese, I realize, and give a little laugh.

Steve Buscemi returns with a gun, wanting my money.

—*I haven't even ordered yet,* I point out.

He wants the money now.

This is silly, I decide, and get up to leave. *One of us is dreaming,* I tell him, *and I think it's me.*

But he holds the gun against my chest. I can feel the cold metal through my thin pajama top.

—*Where's the money?* he says.

—*You were great in* Fargo, I remind him. *This is like that one scene—remember?—you've got the gun, you're all pissed off, and—*

—*Where's the fucking money?*

—*Exactly—there's that face. You're good, you know that? You're really, really . . .*

He begins slowly squeezing the trigger.

If he shoots me I'll never wake up, I realize.

I tell him the money's in my wallet in my pants on the back of a chair in my apartment but if he'll write his address on a napkin . . .

He continues slowly squeezing the trigger.

So now I'm begging: *Oh Jesus, please? Don't? I didn't mean to be here. I never mean to be anywhere. Let me wake up and I promise, I swear to God—*

He shoots me.

I fall backwards slowly, arms wide, eyes closing like a doll's.

I'm dead. Or in a movie. Or dreaming.

I lie very still, waiting to see.

BRIEF ENCOUNTER

I was watching with Marie, on her couch, lights off, my arm around her shoulder. Celia Johnson was getting to me with those big sorrowful eyes and aristocratic accent: "This misery cahn't lahst." And whenever the Rachmaninoff theme music started up, tears immediately sprang to my eyes. I had to work hard not to make any sounds. At one point I gave a sort of whimper—when she tells Trevor Howard, "I want to die"—but I covered it with a cough.

The ending, though, put me over the top. Trevor Howard is gone—they've said goodbye, forever—and Celia Johnson (Laura) is sitting at home with her good kind solid husband Fred who, noticing how miserable she looks over there with her needlepoint, lays aside his crossword puzzle and goes to her, getting down on one knee beside her chair:

"Laura?"

She answers, still far away: "Yes, dear?"

"Whatever your dream was, it wasn't a very happy one, was it."

She's trying not to cry. "No," she says.

"You've been a long way away."

She's trying very hard not to cry. "Yes," she says.

"Thank you for coming back to me," he tells her.

She breaks down: "Oh, Fred."

They embrace, music up.

The End.

"Excuse me," I said, and headed quickly for the bathroom. I locked the door and stood there holding onto the sink, getting a grip on myself, then tossed some water in my face, toweled off and returned to the couch.

Marie had meanwhile turned off the television and switched on a lamp. Her face was bone dry. "You okay?" she asked.

"Fine," I told her. "Had to see a man about a . . ." She was studying me carefully. "What," I said, sitting down again.

"Were you crying?" she asked.

"*No*," I told her, laughing at the notion. "Little bit," I admitted.

She nodded. "Do you always cry at sad movies?"

This was our fifth date, my second time at her apartment, and our first sad movie together. I liked Marie an awful lot, and I was fairly certain she liked me too. We still hadn't slept together but I was hoping to change that tonight. This crying-at-movies, though, could possibly hurt my chances.

"I don't ordinarily cry at movies," I explained, "but sometimes I do get a little teary-eyed if it's not only sad but also very . . . what's the word I want . . . French word . . ."

"Poignant?"

"Exactly. If it's sad in a poignant way, then, yes, I'm liable to shed a tear or two."

She nodded, adding this to her file of things about me. "That's sort of . . . sweet," she said, doubtfully.

"So . . . you don't? Ever?"

"Cry at movies?" She shook her head regretfully.

"Regardless how sad?"

"Or poignant," she added.

I nodded, filing this.

"Does that make me a cold person in your opinion?" she asked, point blank.

"Of course not," I assured her. "Crying at movies. Come on. What is that? Pretty silly. Pretty *foolish*, in fact. Don't you think?"

"Well . . ."

"Do you think it's foolish? You can say."

"I wouldn't say *foolish*, necessarily."

"What *would* you say?"

"A little unusual, that's all. For a guy, anyway."

Stung, trying not to show it, I nodded and looked around—at the crammed bookcase, the basket of mail, the potted plant, the Navaho rug on the wall. "Of course, some people," I said, "some *women* anyway, might find that rather appealing in a guy, crying at movies. Shows he has a, you know, a sensitive nature. A lot of women regard that very highly in a guy."

"I do too," she assured me, and touched my leg. "I just don't think crying at movies necessarily means someone has a sensitive nature."

"Possibly not," I said, nodding some more, stung again. "But let me say this. A *lot* of people—not necessarily me, but a lot of people—might find it just a little bit unusual that a woman could sit through a film so moving, so . . . you know . . ."

"Poignant?"

"So moving, so poignant, without shedding a single tear. Some people might find that a little bit . . . well, troubling."

"Troubling," she said.

I nodded. "Little bit. For a woman. Sure."

"Because I don't fall apart over some sappy, ridiculous—"

"*Sappy?* You thought the movie was—"

"And that hat of hers. Oh, my God."

"Her hat?"

"That was, without a doubt, the silliest-looking—"

"I don't remember any—"

"I was trying so hard not to laugh."

"At her hat?"

"I was trying so hard."

Well, you could see she was hurt—eyes brimming, ready to spill—that was why she was lashing out at Celia Johnson's hat. I said to her, "Marie . . ."

"So why don't you just go," she told me, getting up and marching towards the closet, swiping at her eyes. "I honestly think that would be best." She took my coat off the hanger—then suddenly stepped inside and closed the door on herself.

I stood up. "Marie?"

She didn't answer.

I went over there. "Hey," I said.

She still didn't answer.

I knocked. "You okay in there?"

"Go away please." She was definitely crying now.

"I need my coat," I told her, so she would open the door.

She opened it just enough to drop my coat and quickly closed it again.

I stood there. On our other dates she had seemed like such a levelheaded person, wonderfully so, and now this. "Marie?"

No answer.

"I'm not leaving while you're in there," I told her.

"Suit yourself."

I tried to open the door but she was holding it firmly closed. I tried with both hands but she was strong for a woman and I was weak for a man, and gave up. "Marie, listen," I said. "Are you listening?"

"I'm right here."

"I don't think you're coldhearted, honest to God I really don't. Just because you don't cry at movies? That's ridiculous. Look at me, I cry at them all the time and you're right, it doesn't make me a sensitive person. In fact? I'll tell you a secret, and this is the truth: I never cry over things I *ought* to cry over, things in *real* life, and you know why? I'm not a hundred percent sure about this, but you know what I think? It's because there's no *theme* music in real life. Seriously. I think it's because there's no background music."

She didn't say anything but I could sense her in there listening.

I went further: "I'm going to tell you something, Marie, okay? I've never told this to anyone. At my father's funeral—my own father, his funeral—practically everyone in the whole room was crying their eyes out, except for me. Even standing over the casket, looking down at him—nothing. I remember thinking, *What's wrong with me? Why can't I cry? Why can't I feel anything?* But then, you know what happened? This is the truth. I was standing there with Mike, my brother Mike—he was crying and I was totally dry-eyed, totally ashamed of myself—but then the organist started playing "Amazing Grace," very quietly, very tenderly, and I fell apart. Completely. I started sobbing. Mike had to practically hold me *up*. He had to help me back to my chair. And all the while, Marie—here's the thing—all the while, I remember thinking to myself, *Oh my God, you're enjoying this.*"

I stood there. I felt limp. I had never told that to anyone. Stepping up to the door I leaned my forehead against the wood, closed my eyes—and Marie suddenly opened the door. I staggered backwards, my hands tented over my nose and mouth.

"Oh my God, are you all right?" she said, following me.

"I don't know." I could feel blood.

"Let me see."

I took my hands away.

She covered her nose and mouth.

I covered mine again.

We stood there like that, looking at one another for a long time.

*

So now I've got this permanent little bump on the bridge of my nose. I kind of like it. So does Marie. Sometimes when we're lying in bed together she traces her finger over the place and we talk about that goofy night, years ago now.

Since then, I've discovered Marie cries at quite a variety of things, but still not at movies, no matter how sad or even poignant.

I don't cry at them like I used to. They're just movies, after all. But I have to say, *Brief Encounter* was on TV again recently and it still got to me. Silly hat or not, Celia Johnson is so good in that.